The Living White House

FOREWORD BY MRS. LYNDON B. JOHNSON

INTRODUCTION BY BRUCE CATTON

BY LONNELLE AIKMAN
National Geographic Senior Editorial Staff

White House Historical Association

with the cooperation of the
NATIONAL GEOGRAPHIC SOCIETY
Special Publications Division
Washington, D.C.

THE LIVING WHITE HOUSE

by *Lonnelle Aikman*

Produced as a public service by the Special Publications Division of the

NATIONAL GEOGRAPHIC SOCIETY

Melville Bell Grosvenor, PRESIDENT AND EDITOR

Franc Shor, ASSOCIATE EDITOR, *National Geographic*, AND EDITORIAL DIRECTOR FOR THIS BOOK

SPECIAL PUBLICATIONS STAFF

Robert L. Breeden, EDITOR

Donald J. Crump, ASSISTANT EDITOR AND PICTURE EDITOR

Philip B. Silcott, ASSISTANT TO THE EDITOR

Mary Ann Harrell, RESEARCH

Geraldine Linder, ASSISTANT PICTURE EDITOR

Joseph A. Taney, ART DIRECTOR

Josephine B. Bolt, ASSISTANT ART DIRECTOR

Ronald M. Fisher, PRODUCTION

James R. Whitney, ENGRAVING AND PRINTING

PHOTOGRAPHY: *James P. Blair* and *Joseph J. Scherschel*

EDITORIAL STAFF: *Luba Balko, Margaret Dean, Margaret McKelway, Linda Seeman, Betty Strauss, Peggy Winston*

To Mrs. Lyndon B. Johnson, who inspired this book, the Special Publications Division wishes to express its gratitude. The staff also extends its appreciation to the White House Personnel who assisted during the book's preparation: Elizabeth S. Carpenter, Press Secretary to Mrs. Johnson; Bess Abell, Social Secretary; James R. Ketchum, Curator; and Robert L. Knudsen, Photographer.

Library of Congress Catalog No. 66-30559

COVER: *Beneath Japanese lanterns, the Marine Band plays at a buffet for Presidential Scholars in June, 1966.*

END PAPER: *Radiant gas jets turn the White House to gold as guests arrive for a January reception in 1886, during President Grover Cleveland's first term.*
LIBRARY OF CONGRESS

FRONTISPIECE: *During public visiting hours, schoolboys and their teacher study Samuel F. B. Morse's portrait of Col. William Drayton and other paintings in the Red Room.*

RIGHT: *Old Guard Fife and Drum Corps performs in the East Room for children of diplomats in December, 1965.*
N.G.S. PHOTOGRAPHER JAMES P. BLAIR (ALSO COVER AND FRONTISPIECE)

OVERLEAF: *In the Green Room, Mrs. Lyndon B. Johnson entertains wives of newly assigned American ambassadors.*
NATIONAL GEOGRAPHIC PHOTOGRAPHER JOSEPH J. SCHERSCHEL

Contents

Foreword

MANY YEARS AGO, I stood outside the iron gates of the White House and snapped a photograph of the stately old building gleaming through green shrubbery.

As the wife of a new Texas Congressman, I never imagined that some day I would live on the other side of the fence. Yet even then I felt that this property belonged to me, as it does to every American.

All of us share in the memories that have been accumulating here since 1800, when John and Abigail Adams first moved into this house. Each year and each new administration add more.

A President and his family cannot forget that they have joined the stream of history; that the home they occupy briefly, living their own family life, is also an American showplace where the public is welcomed. Through everything they do runs the consciousness that here throbs the heart of a great and powerful nation.

It is both inspiring and sobering to realize that decisions reached within these walls have shaped our country's development, and will continue to mold its future.

As I go about my daily affairs, I like to recall that the famous men and women who came before us knew the same curious mingling of public and private activities. One moment I have been in a state chamber greeting distinguished world visitors or Members of Congress and the Cabinet (those solution-seekers to the problems of the day); a few minutes later I have found myself curling up with our daughters Lynda and Luci, in one of their bedrooms, talking over their news.

One of the greatest rewards of residing in the White House has been the opportunity to see our children mature in an atmosphere that provokes thought and appreciation of their national heritage.

I remember a time when Lincoln's biographer, Carl Sandburg, and the documentary photographer, Edward Steichen, with their wives, came to tea in the restored Lincoln Room of our second-floor quarters. Lynda, then a college sophomore, quietly absorbed the words of these authorities on Americana—a thrilling experience for a girl intensely involved in the study of history.

As the latest White House family, we have also enjoyed—and learned from—returning members of earlier Presidential families. We have exchanged anecdotes with them, and shown them the changes that we, in our turn, have made here. For every event in this house takes its place, however small, in the continuing saga of the American people.

With the advances in mass communications—and especially in photography—modern Presidents increasingly have shared the White House with the public.

We are profoundly grateful to the National Geographic Society, and to its President and Editor, Melville Bell Grosvenor, for the production of this book as a public service. *The Living White House*, which deals with the personal lives of all our Chief Executives and their families, offers a supplement to the earlier White House guidebook (also produced by the Society) that describes the building and its possessions.

We hope these two books, together, will evoke the long cavalcade of White House occupants who played their very human roles in the story of our country.

Lady Bird Johnson

George Washington, the Presidency behind him,
passes the Executive Mansion on his way home to Mount Vernon.

INTRODUCTION

A Man's Decisions, A Nation's Destiny

By BRUCE CATTON

When a new President of the United States moves into the White House, he enters a dwelling that is home, office, and goldfish bowl all in one. His family must get used to it, he must do the best he can with his job within it and in spite of it. He is never far from crowds or the glare of the limelight, and at times he must surely be the loneliest man in America, when he is called on to sit alone and make a decision that may change the course of world history. He is the people's possession; when he speaks he speaks for them; and the White House has long echoes.

For example, the White House gets part of its tone from the one President who never lived in it—George Washington.

Washington did not especially want to be President. He was, however, the one American who could conceivably be given the job, once the independent country had established its new Constitution, and he took it with the desire to make the new government respected at home and abroad. To do this, he felt that the Presidency itself must be made imposing; it must have not merely authority—which the Constitution offered—but presence. Washington's own towering prestige gave it this, and he saw to it that the trappings of office were appropriate. For an executive mansion he had an imposing town house, first in New York and then in Philadelphia. He held "levees" after the royal manner, with powdered footmen in the entrance hall. He lived in a style intended to prove that the Chief Executive of the United States was a person of great importance.

If he strengthened the office by taking it and by the way he held it, Washington gave it added dignity by the way he gave it up, insisting that the new President and Vice President—John Adams and Thomas Jefferson—precede him from the room in Philadelphia where they had taken the oath of office. His first act as a private citizen was to pay a visit of respect to his successor. On his way home to Mount Vernon, he avoided honors and ceremony whenever he could and acknowledged them gravely when he could not—as when he passed the unfinished President's House by the Potomac, while spectators cheered and the militia fired a salute.

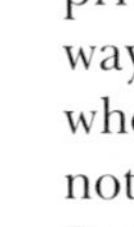

Adams, who moved into the still unfinished house in 1800, carried on the style that Washington had set, and after he moved out in 1801 he grumbled a bit at some of Jefferson's ways. Jefferson, said Adams, had a dozen or more at table every day, and as far as public receptions went "Jefferson's whole eight years was a levee."

Jefferson enjoyed company, and he set a good table—thoughtfully spreading green canvas in the dining room "merely to secure a very handsome floor from grease"—but no President was more fully acquainted with the loneliness that executive responsibility can force upon the country's chief officer. In the spring of 1803 he had to handle one of the most momentous problems that ever came to the White House: the question whether the struggling new nation should suddenly become continental in scope by buying the vast Louisiana country from Napoleon of France.

The United States' western boundary was the Mississippi. Napoleon had acquired the great empty stretch of territory beyond, running all the way to the ill-defined Oregon country in the far northwest. Then, unexpectedly canceling his earlier plans for a New World empire, he offered to sell it to the United States for $15,000,000.

That put it up to Jefferson. He doubted whether the Constitution permitted such a purchase; and in any case, to double the size of the American nation, which was still struggling to digest what it already had, was an extremely venturesome proposition. The President decided to take the plunge. Even before Napoleon made his offer, Jefferson had been making arrangements to send an expedition to explore the west—telling Meriwether Lewis to report on soils, animals, fossils, volcanic appearances, climate, and the Indian nations, including "their language, tradition, monuments,"

Jefferson sends Meriwether Lewis to explore the vast Louisiana country.

President Jackson salutes our Federal Union—and preserves it.

and "peculiarities in their laws, customs & dispositions." Jefferson agreed to buy this huge wilderness sight unseen. Apparently he did not consult his Cabinet; he simply made up his mind, took the responsibility, and, alone in his study, set the little republic on the way to what a later generation would call its manifest destiny—which would not have become manifest at all if the President had not been willing to make the decision.

That is the sort of thing the American President must now and then do—say "yes" or "no" on some matter of the greatest importance, sharing the responsibility with no one, relying entirely on his own judgment and strength.

THIS LONELINESS must have been borne in on James Madison, Jefferson's successor, with especial weight. Madison in 1812 took the responsibility of leading the nation into a war with England. Two years later, British invaders landed in Maryland and swept aside a small band of American defenders that included the President himself. The Redcoats then advanced on the Capital and burned the White House. The result was less disastrous than it seemed; the Capital City recovered, the President returned, the White House was restored, and the war settled for all time the matter of the nation's independence. But on the night he saw the flames, Madison must have had some long, somber thoughts.

In the generation following the War of 1812 the young country grew and changed, and in the process it grew closer to the White House, particularly when Andrew Jackson became President in 1829. Significantly enough, Jackson was the first President who did not come from a well-established family in comfortable circumstances. The day of the tidewater aristocracy was over, and the

"As I would not be a slave, so I would not be a master."—Abraham Lincoln.

"Log Cabin to the White House" legend appeared full-blown. There had been a great increase in population, a great increase in the number of citizens who voted, an expansion of democracy—and, by way of celebration, thousands of people who had not previously set foot inside the White House came to Washington for Jackson's inauguration. Their rowdy exuberance scandalized the well-born and symbolized the fact that from this time on the democracy was going to take a much more alert and personal interest in what happened in the White House than it had before.

Jackson took full advantage of his popularity when South Carolina undertook to nullify a tariff she found unbearable and the question of states' rights seemed to threaten the Union. The country was wondering what stand Jackson would take. Characteristically, he decided to take a bold one, and he made it dramatically clear at a Jefferson Day banquet held in a Washington hotel on April 13, 1830. Sponsors of this affair hoped to commit party leaders to nullification, and gave 24 toasts full of states' rights ideas. When they finally called on the President to speak, he was ready with the toast: "Our *Federal* Union—*It must be preserved.*"

His staunch friend Senator Thomas Hart Benton would write years later that this sentence "was received by the public as a proclamation from the President, to announce a plot against the Union, and to summon the people to its defence." And when the nullifiers continued to talk of secession and Jackson issued a formal proclamation of warning, he carried his point and the threat of civil war receded. He called the people to support their government as only the President could do.

Jackson had given the people a role in the government they had not had before. He openly espoused the spoils system, removing government employees who had been appointed by his predecessors and replacing them with men of his own party. To be sure, the extent to which Jackson did this has been greatly overstated. But adoption of the spoils system gave Jackson and later Presidents a new kind of problem—the necessity of dealing with a great multitude of office seekers. The White House took on a new guise: It was a source of jobs.

FOR DECADES thereafter, the job-hunter was the bane of each President's existence. Applicants thronged the President's office; their letters piled up on his desk. A few might be touching, or funny, or both—Grover Cleveland once got a request from a young man who wrote simply, "The buisnes I am at is Junk buisiness, but I would rather have the buisness in the govment, either in the Cabnet or as watchman." Many applicants were just pesky.

The theory behind the spoils system was simple. Government in those days employed few outright technicians, and as far as the average voter could see most public jobs could be filled by deserving party members as well as by anyone else; and the political organization that had won an election could strengthen itself immeasurably if it could reward the party faithful with places on the payroll. So every President, for generations, had to devote a great deal of his time and energy to the claims of men who believed themselves fully entitled to government posts.

This was especially trying because until 1902 the President's living quarters were on the same floor as his office. In 1861, day after day, anywhere from ten to fifty perspiring political hacks would lie in wait at the door to President Lincoln's office, to press their claims on him when he came out for lunch. Secretary of State William H. Seward wrote at this time that he had to call at the White House two or three times every day, and that whenever he did he found that "the grounds, halls, stairways and closets are filled with applicants, who render ingress and egress difficult." How the weary President could cope with them while he was trying to fight a war is almost beyond imagining. Lincoln himself once remarked that he was like a man who was trying to put out a fire in one part of his house while at the same time he was busy renting rooms in another part.

Wartime, of course, brought innumerable callers who simply wanted the President to intervene in cases where the cumbersome machinery of war ground down on defenseless people. If a soldier was court-martialed for going to sleep on sentry duty, if a politician or editor was arrested for disloyalty real or alleged, if a luckless volunteer found himself unable to collect his pay, if a loyal farmer in secessionist territory found his horses and cows confiscated by an army quartermaster—in hundreds of cases like these, someone was certain to come to the White House to explain the situation and try to get clemency or justice. Small decisions, perhaps, but desperately important to the families concerned.

That all of this pressed on the Commander in Chief with terrible weight is obvious. Yet Lincoln seems to have had in the back of his

From a wheelchair, Theodore Roosevelt intervenes as a coal strike threatens a national crisis.

mind the thought that Washington had had, many years earlier—that the President ran a danger if he let himself become too secluded "by too much reserve and too great a withdrawal." So two or three times a week Lincoln set aside a few hours for visits by all and sundry, and found his office jammed with scores of people who wanted to say a word to the President. He called these sessions his "public opinion baths," and he apparently felt that it was good for him to maintain this close contact with the people whom he was leading through a war. It may have worn him out, but it kept him posted on what the people were thinking.

AND UNDER ALL THESE STRESSES, Lincoln had those solitary moments of far-reaching decision—those moments when the President alone must say the final word and take the final responsibility. The decision to reinforce Fort Sumter, made in the knowledge that this would bring a showdown on the question of peace or war, and the decision to issue the Emancipation Proclamation, committing the nation to a war for human freedom as well as for reunion, were just two of the hard choices he had to make.

Like many other Presidents, Lincoln used his Cabinet when he chose and ignored it when he saw fit. Some Presidents consulted theirs extensively—James Monroe, for instance, held long discussions with his Cabinet before the Monroe Doctrine was framed. But Woodrow Wilson and Franklin D. Roosevelt rarely met with their Cabinets during the two world wars, and Calvin Coolidge, presiding during a much quieter time, liked to limit Cabinet meetings to fifteen minutes.

New advisory bodies and individuals have appeared in recent times, to help the President cope with economic affairs, to help him understand new developments in science, and to explain new uses of technology, for over the years the role of the government—and its Chief Executive—has enormously increased. True, one source of pressure diminished after the death of Garfield, who was badgered by office seekers until a demented and disappointed applicant shot him. Then the public demand for civil service reform became irresistible; and as more and more jobs became classified under civil service, the clamor for patronage became less widespread and strident.

The President gained another immeasurable benefit when the new executive wing was added at the west end of the White House in 1902. No longer did the Chief Magistrate have to wade through a mob when he tried to walk from the place where he worked to the place where he lived. At last the office and the home were physically separated.

Still, the man who lives in the White House must find the cares of office as inescapable as his own flesh and bone. To talk with a friend who has a new baby to welcome or a death to mourn, he may have to snatch moments from planning an international conference. When he greets his guests at a party, he may have to hide his concern over crises abroad; when he has shaken hands with hundreds of fellow citizens, the ache in his fingers may be forgotten for the aching anxiety of spirit that a moment's news can bring; and when he wrestles with dilemmas of state, the stress of circumstance may wring vitality out of him as the swirl and weight of storm-run surf twist strength out of a swimmer.

Many of the great Presidential decisions have come in problems that no Chief Executive could evade, because the Constitution requires him to accept them as his responsibility—he may act boldly, or he may temporize, but he must face the issue or break his oath. In other cases, the President has decided on his own initiative to intervene in a situation of great public urgency—once a President in a wheel chair decided to take an active part in settling a costly labor dispute.

President Truman's fateful decision: to use the atomic bomb in World War II.

Coal miners had gone on strike and stayed out for months. The men who owned the mines refused to negotiate, the coal piles were going down and prices were going up, and winter was coming on. Then the President announced that he would take a hand, and invited the opposing parties to confer in his presence. This was Theodore Roosevelt—not Franklin—he had injured his left leg in a carriage accident, and the "White House conference" took place in a temporary office at 22 Jackson Place while workmen put up the new West Wing. On October 3, 1902, T.R. opened the meeting by disclaiming any official right or duty to intervene, and appealed to both groups to compose their differences to "meet the crying needs of the people." The miners' leader, John Mitchell, spoke simply enough, suggesting that the President name a commission to settle the questions at issue. A White House staff member said later that the President would have been justified in throwing chairs at the owners, who accused him of making "a grandstand play" and refused to make any concessions at all. That night Roosevelt wrote gloomily that he had failed.

As it turned out, he had succeeded. The owners had antagonized many of their most conservative supporters by their behavior at the conference and afterward. Roosevelt continued to press for a solution, and soon it became clear that public opinion approved his unprecedented actions. The owners gave in and agreed to let the President name an arbitration commission. The miners went back to work, and that crisis was over.

Since 1902 the White House has seen many other changes designed to make it safer and more comfortable as a home and more efficient as a place in which to work. It remains a place where a family carries on the day-to-day business of living, and also a place where one man has to make decisions—as Harry Truman had to do when he learned that the atom bomb was in his hands. He had to weigh the unknown lives an invasion of Japan would cost, and the unknown effects of this mysterious new weapon; and he knew that nobody else in the world could say what was going to be done with it. Or as John F. Kennedy had to do when he learned that missiles were being set up in Cuba. In one discussion with his advisers, he said simply: "Once we walk out of this room, people can start to get killed." For one thing he knew with certainty was this: The President of the United States was not the only man who could order the use of nuclear weapons if things came to the worst.

In recent decades the world has drawn much closer to the White House. Perhaps it would not be too much to say that the heads of foreign nations take as alert an interest in what happens there as the governors of the several states did in the old days. Still, the White House is a peculiarly American institution. If it reflects the personality of the man who occupies it, it also reflects the total personality of the people who put him there. It is their own special possession and symbol, embodying what they have hoped for and dreamed of and want to live up to.

Facing the Cuban missile crisis, President Kennedy weighs the chances for peace.

I

Hail to the Chief

FOR 166 YEARS every President has led two lives in the White House—his own and his country's. Indeed, the perpetual interplay between the human joys and sorrows of its tenants and the great events of a growing, changing nation is what makes the story of this house at once so appealing and so exciting.

It is charming to recall, for instance, that widower Thomas Jefferson relaxed from the cares of the young Republic by playing his fiddle, and training his pet mockingbird to take food from his lips.

And that the marriage of James and Dolley Madison—who were burned out of the Executive Mansion in the War of 1812—was one of the happiest in history. Statuesque Dolley once wrote of the small, studious President as her "darling little husband." He said that a conversation with her was as refreshing as a long walk in the park.

Abraham Lincoln found relief from Civil War problems in chuckling over the pranks of his boy Tad, who once stole the President's spectacles for a circus performance in the attic—admission five cents.

Scholarly Woodrow Wilson, whose eloquence moved audiences to tears and cheers in World War I, delighted in showing off his skill as a vaudeville comic.

And every Christmas Eve throughout the Great Depression and World War II, Franklin Roosevelt gathered his large family around him for the traditional reading from Dickens's *Christmas Carol.*

Not all Presidential families, of course, found their personal lives overshadowed by national crisis and

IN A HISTORIC PROCESSION, *President and Mrs. Johnson escort Chancellor Ludwig Erhard of West Germany to the East Room. There Cabinet officers and diplomats wait as the White House resounds to the Marine Band's stirring tribute, "Hail to the Chief." Vice President and Mrs. Humphrey stand beside a bust of President Washington. Lynda Bird Johnson wears a white gown for the state dinner at Yuletide in 1965.*

NATIONAL GEOGRAPHIC PHOTOGRAPHER JOSEPH J. SCHERSCHEL

PLURIBUS

danger. But all left with the White House the mark and the memory of themselves and their times. George Washington, who served in New York and Philadelphia before the Capital moved to the Federal City, chose the future building's site and approved its design—thus bequeathing to his countrymen a graceful 18th-century mansion with a superlative view.

Beginning with John Adams, the nation's First Home has reflected America's changing manners and tastes, just as the issues facing each new Chief Executive mirrored the country's progress as it grew from a shaky union of coastal states to a continent-spanning giant of wealth and power.

Today, the President's House, surrounded by 18 acres of rolling green in the heart of busy Washington, still has the serene, detached look of a rural English estate.

Nothing could be further from reality. Behind the big white pillars, a thousand-and-one activities go on daily to ensure the orderly handling of official papers, the routing of mail and visitors, the process of domestic routine, and the preparations for a constant round of social functions.

Nowhere on earth does the hot, searching spotlight of public attention beat down more fiercely and ceaselessly than on this house. Nearly 2,000 accredited reporters, including some 50 regularly assigned to cover the President and First Lady, stand ready to flash news around the globe.

Moreover, nearly two million tourists a year now visit the mansion's stately display

ROBERT L. KNUDSEN (ABOVE)

SPACIOUS ROOMS *on the second and third floors provide a place for members of the First Family to entertain informally, visit among themselves, or simply relax as Mrs. Johnson does here in the West Sitting Hall. Until Theodore Roosevelt added the West Wing in 1902, White House residents shared the second floor with callers who waited to see the President. The addition afforded more offices for the Chief Executive as well as a measure of privacy for his family.*

rooms, while the nation's business is carried on, unseen, around them. In the first few years of the Lyndon Johnson administration tourists numbered well over four million—or more than the entire population of the United States when George Washington took office.

This fascination that draws Americans to the White House may come partly from awe of the power it embodies and the knowledge that decisions made here affect their destiny and that of the world.

But there is a deeper and more intimate feeling that springs from the link between the citizens of a republic and the man they choose to be their supreme leader.

No other elected official is so directly answerable to and responsible for the welfare of all the people. Their problems are his problems; his home is theirs.

"I never forget," President Franklin Roosevelt said, "that I live in a house owned by all the American people. . . ."

Each morning, Tuesday through Saturday, from ten o'clock to twelve, the visiting public forms long lines outside the White House grounds, waiting to walk through and inspect their property.

Surging along the ground-floor corridors, they climb a marble stairway to the ceremonial floor. A delightful and surprising spectacle awaits them.

The five state chambers, opening one into another from the gold-draped East Room to the Green, Blue, and Red Rooms, and the State Dining Room, are furnished in early American styles used when the house was young. On their walls, almost covering them, hangs a unique collection of portraits of Presidents and their wives.

The whole effect is one of empty stage sets on which a 19th-century play is about to begin. But the effect is misleading. Far from being merely museum exhibits, these rooms form part of the living White House.

No sooner have the tourists departed than a corps of cleaners, dusters, and floor polishers rushes in to ready them for the day's scheduled events.

In the dining hall where visitors from Wisconsin or Florida passed only shortly before, President Johnson may preside at a stag lunch arranged to discuss some vital national issue with a group of newspaper editors or civil rights leaders. In the Red or Green Room a little later, Mrs. Johnson

IN THE WEST WING, *the President confers with members of his official family. The complex demands of government bring heads of executive departments and other advisers to the conference table in the Cabinet Room. In his private office (above) Mr. Johnson consults with President Mohammed Ayub Khan of Pakistan in December, 1965. Here the Chief Executive meets staff members, leaders of industry and labor, resident ambassadors, and statesmen visiting from abroad.*

PEACEFUL TRANSFER OF POWER: *In the American tradition, President Dwight D. Eisenhower and President-elect John F. Kennedy leave the White House together for the inauguration at the Capitol.*

THANK YOU, AND GOODBYE. *President and Mrs. Eisenhower exchange farewells with members of the White House staff on the morning of January 20, 1961.*

PRESIDENT KENNEDY, *the youngest man ever elected to lead his country, reviews his inaugural parade. Beneath the Presidential Seal marches the Connecticut Governor's Foot Guard, descended from colonial militia.*

may serve tea to a literary group consulting on the White House Library. Or still later, both the President and First Lady may stand in the oval Blue Room to greet 1,000 guests at one of the official receptions.

The White House puts on its most glamorous performance, however, at the state dinners given for visiting chiefs of state and heads of government.

Imagine yourself one of a hundred or more select guests, including the Secretary of State and other high government officials. Wearing your most ravishing evening gown—or best dinner jacket—you arrive at the designated entrance, check your wraps in the Diplomatic Reception Room, and follow the tourist route up the marble stairs to the main floor. There you receive a table card, showing your place at dinner.

The red-coated Marine Band—the President's own since 1801—is seated in the Entrance Foyer. It plays a gay melody as an officer in dress uniform, one of the White House social aides, escorts you to the East Room. An aide at the door announces you; others welcome you as you join a line to greet your host. While you are chatting, the President and his wife, with their guests of honor and entourage, are descending the grand stairway. Before them marches the color guard, with the flags of the President and of the United States.

Suddenly you hear the musical salute, ruffles and flourishes. An aide announces the President, his wife, and the guests of honor. The band begins the triumphant

LEE BATTAGLIA (BELOW) AND EDWARD CLARK

march, "Hail to the Chief," surely one of the most stirring airs ever composed. At its first note the aides snap to attention.

Walking between the colors set in standards at either side of the East Room door, the President's party forms a receiving line inside. You pass along it to be presented to your hosts and the state guests.

When all have been greeted, the Marine Band strikes up another march. The President offers his arm to the ranking woman guest, and leads the way to the dining room, followed by the First Lady on the arm of the ranking gentleman. As you step along the red-carpeted corridor, you are on your way to sup with history.

More often than not, such glittering international functions still make history. When two chiefs of state dine together and exchange traditional toasts, their remarks reveal current attitudes and policies that may mark the course of world diplomacy.

In fact, virtually all entertaining at the White House, except the most personal gatherings with friends and relatives, involves the nation's official business.

"... even at a ceremonial dinner and in every hour of leisure," Dwight D. Eisenhower remarked after his first four years on the job, "the old saying is true, 'A President never escapes from his office.'"

Yet the post that Jefferson described as "a splendid misery" has never lacked candidates. Calvin Coolidge dryly observed, when warned of the dangerous condition of the mansion's roof, that he presumed there were plenty of others who would be willing to take the risk.

The 35 men who have taken on the nation's toughest assignment have varied as much as the country in background and advantages. Together they stand as a testimonial to the democratic idea that every American boy has a chance to reach the top.

Andrew Jackson and Lincoln grew up in frontier country. Andrew Johnson, whose wife taught him to read, started out as a

DAILY GRAPHIC, MARCH 7, 1877

SECRET OATH: *Chief Justice Morrison R. Waite administers the oath of office to Rutherford B. Hayes in the Red Room, March 3, 1877. President Grant (left) and Secretary of State Hamilton Fish (shown at right but not in fact present) had advised this procedure because the electoral vote was disputed, and because March 4—then the lawful inauguration day—fell on Sunday.*

NATIONAL GEOGRAPHIC ARTIST ROBERT W. NICHOLSON

WITH A SINGLE CANDLE *to light his way, President Franklin Pierce gropes up the stairs on his first night in the mansion. No servants answered his call; he and his secretary found all the second-floor rooms in disorder. A troubled term of office followed this disheartening beginning.*

N. C. WYETH FOR PENNSYLVANIA RAILROAD, COURTESY SMITHSONIAN INSTITUTION

GEORGE WASHINGTON *inspects the unfinished President's House with architect James Hoban, on a visit to the Federal City (as he chose to call it). He wanted public buildings that "in size, form, and elegance, shou'd look beyond the present day," and thought the Chief Executive's mansion should be expanded when the "wealth, population, and importance" of the country "shall stand upon much higher ground than they do at present." He died before the government moved from Philadelphia in 1800, but Mrs. Washington lived to send a servant to her successor, Abigail Adams, with a gift of venison, an invitation to Mount Vernon, and a message of love.*

tailor. Warren Harding was a newspaper publisher, Herbert Hoover an engineer.

At least 20 Presidents had practiced law; many served as State Governors, Members of Congress, Cabinet officers. Eleven were generals, from George Washington to Dwight Eisenhower. Several, like Woodrow Wilson, had been college professors. One, William Howard Taft, went on to become Chief Justice of the United States—the only man to hold both those high posts.

Few state residences in the world have been home to so many different types of leaders as has the White House. Their personalities and statements color the American story and language.

"Speak softly and carry a big stick," calls up the dynamic career and much-cartooned face of Theodore Roosevelt.

The phrase about making the world "safe for democracy" brings to mind Woodrow Wilson's hopeful, ringing words in his War Message to Congress in 1917.

Out of Franklin Roosevelt's era come a dozen other memorable quotations—among them, "the forgotten man," "the arsenal of democracy," "the four freedoms."

And few state residences have seen such a regular, peaceable exchange of masters. It started when John and Abigail Adams came to the new Federal Capital created in the woods and fields by the Potomac. In that bleak November of 1800, Adams's term had but four months to go. It was neither a happy ending for the couple, nor an auspicious beginning for the Capital.

The Federalist President was bitterly disappointed over his defeat by Jefferson's "radical" party. Mrs. Adams was shocked at the state of the huge, damp, unfinished "President's Palace," as many called it.

". . . shiver, shiver," she wrote her daughter. ". . . surrounded by forests, can you believe that wood is not to be had, because people cannot be found to cut and cart it!"

"The principal stairs are not up . . ." Mrs. Adams complained. There were not enough lamps. With "not the least fence, yard, or

BUYING HIS OWN *groceries, William Henry Harrison shops at the Center Market in early March, 1841. The President carried his purchases home in a basket, and if he met a friend on the way, might invite him to stop in for breakfast at the Executive Mansion.*

DAMP CLOTHES *and damp plaster: the East Room in Abigail Adams's time. Here, her little granddaughter Susanna helps her supervise as a servant hangs the family washing.*

PAINTING BY GORDON PHILLIPS (BELOW) AND F. W. BROUARD

other convenience without," she hung the Presidential laundry to dry in the "great unfinished audience-room," now the elegant East Room.

That practical solution to her wash-day problem would give Abigail a lasting place in domestic annals, though at the time she warned her daughter, "You must keep all this to yourself, and . . . say . . . the situation is beautiful, which is true." In all fairness, she admitted, she had a fine view of the river, and the house was "upon a grand and superb scale."

In fact, John and Abigail Adams left a personal heritage of dignity and integrity with the buff-colored sandstone building later called the White House.

To those who would follow, President Adams also left a generous wish, a benediction that Franklin Roosevelt, many years later, would inscribe on the mantel in the State Dining Room. You can see it there today. Taken from a letter written on Adams's second night in the house, it reads:

"I Pray Heaven to Bestow
The Best of Blessings on
THIS HOUSE
and on All that shall hereafter
Inhabit it. May none but Honest
and Wise Men ever rule under This Roof."

II Hospitality: Toasts,

Teas, and Tomahawks

SOCIAL LIFE at the White House follows a rhythm all its own. Season after season, its events come and go like an endlessly spinning merry-go-round.

Through the years, the wheel's turn has brought Indian chiefs, movie stars, and astronauts; queens whose jewels outshone the sparkling chandeliers, and young princes and princesses who danced the latest steps—from quadrille to frug—at balls given in their honor.

In December, 1965, President and Mrs. Johnson invited 150 children from local welfare institutions to their annual Christmas party. Their daughter Luci, acting as hostess, distributed toys and goodies after the small guests had listened spellbound in the East Room to lilting arrangements of classical music created for youngsters by the noted Swedish pianist, Kabi Laretei.

No two administrations have ever entertained in quite the same fashion. Depending on the Presidential family and current customs, White House hospitality has ranged from stiffly formal to gaily casual. It has been by turns elegant, flamboyant, prim, extravagant, and, in sad times, slowed to funeral cadence.

As host and hostess for their country, early Presidents and First Ladies used this hospitality to promote the nation's interests and underscore its philosophy.

John and Abigail Adams—firm in their belief that the head of the new Republic was due as much ceremony as any monarch—carried on in Washington the stately social rituals begun by President and Mrs. Washington in New York and Philadelphia.

At their weekly levees, or receptions, Mrs. Adams received the Capital's elite—including haughty European diplomats—from a regally seated position. Her husband, standing beside her in black velvet coat and knee breeches, silver buckles and lace, bowed gravely to each newcomer.

President Jefferson, with his faith in equality, changed all that. As he put it, he "buried" the "levees, birthdays, royal parades" of his predecessor. Instead he offered two public receptions—come one, come all—on New Year's Day and the Fourth of July. Disdaining official precedence even in seating dinner guests, Jefferson introduced a "pell-mell" system that outraged sticklers for arrangement by rank.

At one dinner, British Minister Anthony Merry became so indignant when his wife was seated after the Spanish minister, and he had to find a place for himself, that he tried to make an international incident of it. Though Merry's government took no action on what he reported as an insult to British majesty, the diplomat and his wife never again dined at the President's house.

But Jefferson's informality only highlighted the fact that the mansion's second master brought to it the manners and tastes of an aristocrat, gourmet, and intellectual.

At his small parties, attended by some of the wisest men and loveliest women of his time, he served fine wines and imported delicacies prepared by his French chef.

Jefferson's interests and studies encompassed the universe, from astronomy, anthropology, and architecture to farming, music, and history. And it was this enormous erudition that the late President John F. Kennedy recalled in his famous toast at a dinner for 29 Nobel Prize winners.

His guests, said Mr. Kennedy, represented "the most extraordinary collection of talent, of human knowledge, that has ever been gathered together at the White House—with the possible exception of when Thomas Jefferson dined alone."

Jefferson's open house on New Year's Day became a tradition lasting through 1930. After that, the crush of visitors forced President and Mrs. Hoover to call a halt.

ANOTHER Jefferson innovation has never flagged—the democratic handshake he substituted for Adams's formal bow. So enthusiastic was the public response that no successor has dared, or wanted, to abandon it, despite the penalty of sore knuckles when thousands of hands reach for the privilege.

James K. Polk, so thin that he was once described as the "merest tangible fraction of a President," devised a method of his own for avoiding a painful grip. ". . . when I observed a strong man approaching," he explained, "I generally took advantage of him by being a little quicker . . . and seizing him by the top of his fingers, giving him a hearty shake. . . ."

President Lincoln shook hands with guests for three full hours at the traditional

◀ **GRACE AND GLITTER:** *the East Room today. Dancers of Harkness House for Ballet Arts perform "Classical Symphony" at the dedication of a new portable stage, especially designed to match the decor of the ballroom and presented to the White House as a gift in September, 1965.*

NATIONAL GEOGRAPHIC PHOTOGRAPHER JOSEPH J. SCHERSCHEL

NATIONAL GEOGRAPHIC PHOTOGRAPHER JOSEPH J. SCHERSCHEL

RITUALS OF DIPLOMACY *still bring Indians of America to the White House, as in John Adams's time. Above,* Gahan*—mountain spirits revered by the Apache—wield symbols of lightning. Students from Santa Fe gave this performance for President Maurice Yameogo of Upper Volta, and his wife, guests of state in March, 1965. Below, a French artist imagines Lincoln and visiting chiefs conducting a dignified interview, and carefully includes "les tomahawks."*

VOYAGE PITTORESQUE ET ANECDOTIQUE DANS LE NORD ET LE SUD DES ÉTATS-UNIS D'AMÉRIQUE, BY OSCAR COMETTANT

reception on January 1, 1863, before going upstairs to his office to sign the Emancipation Proclamation.

With the official copy spread on the Cabinet table before him, he dipped his pen in the ink and paused. Looking at Secretary of State William H. Seward, he said: "I never ... felt more certain that I was doing right, than I do in signing this paper. But ... my arm is stiff and numb. Now, this signature is one that will be closely examined, and if they find my hand trembled, they will say 'he had some compunctions.' But, any way, it is going to be done!"

Then, carefully and slowly, he wrote the bold "Abraham Lincoln" we see at the end of the document.

Curiously, one Chief Executive who really enjoyed hand-shaking was the taciturn New Englander, Calvin Coolidge. In his administration, White House doors were still thrown open daily, just before lunch, to all who wished to greet the President.

"On one occasion I shook hands with nineteen hundred in thirty-four minutes ..." Mr. Coolidge recalled in his autobiography. "Instead of a burden, it was a pleasure and a relief to meet people in that way and listen to their greeting, which was often a benediction."

PERLEY'S REMINISCENCES (BELOW) AND ILLUSTRATED LONDON NEWS, JUNE 16, 1860

FIRST ENVOYS *from Imperial Japan bow to President Buchanan and his Cabinet before presenting their credentials on May 17, 1860. "In size and extravagance of embroidery" their robes were "worthy the occasion," wrote a reporter. Visiting the Capital to exchange ratifications of a commercial treaty, the Japanese carried their documents in a black lacquer "treaty box," earlier borne along Pennsylvania Avenue "in a square cage."*

No one delighted more in living at the White House—or dispensed warmer hospitality—than did sunny-hearted Dolley Madison, wife of the fourth President. Arriving in 1809, she was already familiar with the big, stately house, having often acted as hostess for the widowed Jefferson when her husband served as Secretary of State. Without her gaiety and high spirits, agreed Jefferson and his private secretary, Meriwether Lewis, they felt "like two mice in a church."

Dolley's good nature was seldom ruffled. To the wife of a disgruntled diplomat, who had sniffed that the Madisons' bountiful offerings seemed "more like a harvest-home supper, than the entertainment of a Secretary of State," she had the devastating retort that the "profusion so repugnant to foreign customs arose from the happy circumstance of the abundance and prosperity in our country. . . ."

As HOSTESS of the White House in her own right after "the great little Madison" went on to the Presidency, Dolley gave lavish dinners and balls. Washington Irving wrote of "the blazing splendor" of her drawing room, refurbished in vivid yellow. In "that centre of attraction," said a lady who knew her well, one saw "all these whom fashion, fame, beauty, wealth or talents, have render'd celebrated."

When the President called Cabinet meetings, Dolley entertained the wives. Leaving political talk to her quietly brilliant husband, she welcomed both Federalist and Republican leaders. She served refreshments to all callers—seed cake and hot bouillon in winter, punch in summer.

In 1812 she arranged the mansion's first wedding—the nuptials of her lovely, widowed sister, Lucy Payne Washington, and "the estimable & amiable" Supreme Court Justice, Thomas Todd.

Reacting, perhaps, to the subdued dress of a Quaker girlhood, Dolley Madison reveled in bright finery. Already tall, she added to her height by wearing flamboyant evening turbans, and accentuated her vibrant personality with rich silks and satins imported from Paris.

But the mansion's "Golden Age," as some called the Madison tenure, was destined to go up in flames during the War of 1812.

The war had begun five months before Madison's election to a second term. Two years later, on a hot August day in 1814, the British landed troops in Maryland. The President and members of his Cabinet galloped out to join the American force assembled near Bladensburg to meet the invaders. As the battle began, Madison staunchly sat his horse in sight of the front line, while enemy rockets fell around him.

Meantime, Mrs. Madison had remained at the White House to pack state papers and valuables, and "be ready at a moment's warning," as she wrote her sister in an hour-by-hour account of the ordeal, "to enter my carriage and leave the city."

Dolley watched anxiously through a spyglass for her husband's return. Occasionally she turned away to add to her letter. "I am still here within sound of the cannon!" she wrote at three o'clock, August 24. "Two messengers covered with dust, come to bid me fly; but I wait for him."

When it finally became clear that there was no other course, Mrs. Madison prepared to leave. But first she rescued Gilbert Stuart's full-length painting of George Washington that now hangs in the East Room. In a last note to her sister, she explained how she saved the famous portrait: "Our kind friend, Mr. Carroll, has come to hasten my departure, and is in a very bad humor with me because I insist on waiting until the large picture of Gen. Washington is secured, and it requires to be unscrewed from the wall. This process was found too tedious for these perilous moments; I have ordered the frame to be broken, and the canvas taken out; it is done. . . ."

Dolley Madison's flight with the nation's precious possessions came none too soon. That night the British, having brushed aside the Bladensburg defenders, marched into Washington and set fire to the White House, Capitol, and other public buildings.

When they withdrew, after a sudden terrifying storm that struck the city the next

IN THE STATE DINING ROOM, *Mrs. Johnson welcomes Japanese guests at a reception in November, 1965. Earlier that day, the First Lady honored an act of friendship by Japan and continued her program of beautification for the Capital. She and Mrs. Ryuji Takeuchi, wife of the Ambassador, planted two flowering cherry trees near the Washington Monument—part of 3,800 saplings, the latest gift from Japan. Mrs. William Howard Taft planted the first cherry tree beside the Tidal Basin in 1912.*

NATIONAL GEOGRAPHIC PHOTOGRAPHER JOSEPH J. SCHERSCHEL

afternoon, the President's House was a dripping, blackened shell.

The Madisons never returned to it. While reconstruction dragged on, they spent their remaining two-and-a-half years in residences rented by the government.

Even after James Monroe's 1817 inaugural, six months passed before the Presidential family could move into the restored building, now painted a glistening white.

Though no one knew it then, the dazzling new front—like the elegantly carved and gilded furniture and bric-a-brac bought by Monroe in France—heralded a return to an earlier social order.

The first hint came at the New Year's reception of 1818, when the President arranged an elaborate ceremony to greet the Capital's foreign diplomats before the usual throngs were admitted. From then on, pomp and protocol reigned. Monroe, like Washington and Adams, hoped to win greater respect from Europe's rulers by placing their ministers "upon much the same footing... of form and ceremony," he said, as that required of American ministers at European courts.

Gone were the days when diplomats could drop by casually on business or pleasure. They came by invitation only, or after requesting a formal audience.

On the distaff side, First Lady Elizabeth Monroe refused to continue the exhausting practice of making first calls or returning them. Her married daughter, Eliza Hay, who lived at the White House with her husband, carried on a feud of her own with diplomatic-corps wives over the etiquette of paying calls.

After the Madisons' easy accessibility, the abrupt change infuriated local society. In retaliation, the city's feminine leaders boycotted the Monroes' "at homes."

"The drawing-room of the President was opened last night to a 'beggarly row of empty chairs,'" wrote Mrs. William Winston Seaton, wife of a prominent Washington newspaper editor. "Only five females attended, three of whom were foreigners."

The teapot tempest steamed again over plans for the wedding of pretty little Maria Monroe, not quite 17, to her mother's nephew and the President's secretary, Samuel Lawrence Gouverneur. Though the Capital was agog at the prospect of seeing the first White House marriage of a President's daughter, the family decided to make it a private affair. Even foreign diplomats were passed over, and advised "to take no notice" of the event.

"The New York style was adopted..." Mrs. Seaton commented tartly. "Only the attendants, the relations, and a few old

GUEST OF HONOR *in the President's Dining Room, British Prime Minister Harold Wilson leans forward to hear Secretary of State Dean Rusk report on problems of Asia and Africa. Ambassador Sir Patrick Dean sits at the President's left. The wallpaper of the second-floor room portrays a less amicable period of British-American relations—the Revolutionary War.*

friends of the bride and groom witnessed the ceremony. . . ."

Residents of the Executive Mansion, however, have a built-in advantage over all challengers. Gradually, Washington society accepted Monroe etiquette and returned.

More important, future First Ladies would bless Mrs. Monroe for freedom from time-consuming sociabilities. And the President who coolly kept the diplomats at a distance was the President who proclaimed the Monroe Doctrine—warning the powers of Europe against attempting further colonization in the Western Hemisphere.

No Presidential couple brought longer and more varied diplomatic experience to the White House than did Monroe's successor, John Quincy Adams, and his wife Louisa. John Quincy, son of the first President to reside here, had served his country at courts in Russia, the Netherlands, and England. Louisa, born in London of an American father and an English mother, was a polished hostess who played the harp and was well read in Greek, French, and English literature.

The Adamses continued the Monroe style of formal entertaining. Waiters, edging through crowded state rooms, held high large trays of ice cream, coffee, tea,

NATIONAL GEOGRAPHIC PHOTOGRAPHER JOSEPH J. SCHERSCHEL

"**LINCOLN'S LAST RECEPTION.**" *After his second inauguration, the President greets Mrs. Ulysses S. Grant. Vice President Andrew Johnson stands at his side. Contrary to this contemporary print, neither Johnson nor Mrs. Grant attended, and General Grant (behind her) had remained with his army in Virginia.*

"**SO MYSTERIOUS** *and so shocking . . ." As Lincoln had dreamed, mourners gather in the East Room. Artist G. White erred in details of the funeral—Mary Lincoln, shown veiled, did not attend it—but he conveyed its rigid formality and its bitter sorrow. Mourning ribbons like the one at right quoted the President: "I have said nothing but what I am willing to live by, and if it be the pleasure of Almighty God, to die by."*

cakes, jellies, wines and liqueurs, plus West Indies fruits as a special treat in winter.

A conscientious New Englander, John Quincy Adams opened his doors every fortnight to public levees that taxed his strength and patience.

"This evening was the sixth drawing-room," he wrote in his diary after one such affair. "Very much crowded; sixteen Senators, perhaps sixty members of the House of Representatives, and multitudes of strangers . . . these parties are becoming more and more insupportable. . . ."

Like the Monroes, the Adams family provided a historic wedding. In 1828, John

Adams – son of John Quincy and namesake of his famous grandfather – exchanged vows here with his cousin Mary Catherine Hellen. The ceremony took place in what was later called the Blue Room, then decorated in crimson and gold. It was historic because young Adams was the first, and so far the only, President's son to take a bride in the Executive Mansion.

Father Adams had at first withheld his consent to the match, probably because gay, fickle Mary Catherine had flirted earlier with John's two brothers. But the wedding reception offered a festive event in a bitter election year. Even the staid President forgot his cares, and danced the Virginia Reel.

Yet Adams's defeat was already in the air. With it would come the end of an era. The first six Presidents, leaders of the Revolution and statesmen rich in diplomatic experience, had represented the eastern aristocracy of land and intellect.

The decisive victory of Andrew Jackson – veteran Indian fighter, hero of the Battle of New Orleans, and frontier property owner – put into the executive saddle the favorite son of the new and booming West.

Jackson's followers swept into Washington for the inauguration of the "People's President" with the zest of ranch hands celebrating on Saturday night. Or as one of his biographers said, "It was like the inundation of northern barbarians into Rome."

After the Capitol ceremony, the crowds moved on to the White House reception, where some stood in muddy boots on satin chairs while eager handshakers pressed Jackson against the wall. In their rush for food and drink they broke china and glasses until attendants could direct them to tubs of punch on the lawn. The President eluded the mob's joyous embrace only by slipping out and spending the night at Gadsby's hotel, then nicknamed the "Wigwam."

If Jackson's administration exploded with a rude bang, "Old Hickory" himself

RALPH E. BECKER COLLECTION OF POLITICAL AMERICANA, SMITHSONIAN INSTITUTION (LOWER LEFT) AND KIPLINGER COLLECTION

WIDE WORLD (ABOVE) AND CECIL B. STOUGHTON

MARTYRED PRESIDENT, *John F. Kennedy lies in the crape-hung East Room on a black catafalque, where Lincoln's body had lain almost a century before. On this rain-shrouded November 23, 1963, the nation's leaders mourned here, and an honor guard stood rigid in grief.*

BLACK-VEILED *Jacqueline Kennedy walks erect and resolute, with the dignity that won her the enduring respect of the world, as she follows her husband's body from the White House. Behind her followed the greatest assemblage of global leaders ever to appear in the Capital.*

proved far from a backwoods bumpkin. Accustomed to fine surroundings in his Tennessee plantation home, the President soon took steps to alter the shabby state in which he found the mansion—a result of Adams's unpopularity with Congress.

During his eight years of office, Jackson obtained nearly $50,000 in appropriations to add the North Portico and to furnish and equip the house.

For the first time, the renovations provided for the complete and handsome furnishing of the great East Room. The President ordered the Monroe chairs upholstered, with the remark, according to a newspaper, that they would keep the people from "standing upon their legs as they do before kings and emperors."

Official entertaining also took on magnificent proportions, with the Adamses' French chef staying on to see that the tables groaned with every kind of food a lush new land could produce.

But Andrew Jackson had come to the White House in mourning. Never would he be free of the grief caused by the loss of his beloved wife Rachel, who had died of a heart attack shortly after his election.

Rachel's death, he brooded, was due to malicious campaign gossip that had revived the 33-year-old scandal of their marriage under the mistaken belief that her first husband had gotten a divorce. Even though the Jacksons had remarried after the divorce was granted, political enemies made much of the matter. "May God Almighty forgive her murderers, as I know she forgave them," he said. "I never can."

Thus the President was ready to wage what the Capital called a petticoat war in defense of the reputation of another woman whom he felt to be similarly maligned.

When the wives of high government officials refused to receive pretty Peggy O'Neale Eaton, daughter of a Washington innkeeper and wife of the Secretary of

War, Jackson put pressure on their husbands. All but one of his Cabinet members resigned before the war ended, with John Eaton taking Peggy to his new assignment as American minister to Spain.

President Jackson's last levee in the Executive Mansion had something of the popular excitement of his first. As he was about to leave office, in 1837, he accepted the gift of a fourteen-hundred-pound cheese. Setting it up in the north hall, he invited the public to share it at a celebration of George Washington's birthday.

People from far and near accepted with pleasure. What they didn't eat, they dropped on the floor and stepped on.

The spectacle—and the lingering smell—some said, explained the less hospitable ways of the next President, Martin Van Buren, Jackson's choice to inherit his mantle.

As the third widower to enter the White House, President Van Buren brought along four eligible sons—enough to put Washington matchmakers on their mettle.

One succeeded. Dolley Madison—now an aging widow but still alert to romance—introduced the President's eldest son Abraham to Angelica Singleton, a distant relative of hers then visiting the Capital. The marriage that followed did not deprive the President of a son. Rather, it gave him a beautiful and charming young

FRANK LESLIE'S ILLUSTRATED NEWSPAPER, LIBRARY OF CONGRESS

daughter to act as his official hostess.

Martin Van Buren was less lucky in other ways. The "Little Magician," as Jackson's clever Vice President was nicknamed, had lost popularity by discontinuing the regular public receptions. While the country suffered a severe depression, his enemies pictured him as living and entertaining luxuriously, despising the common people.

Congressman Charles Ogle of Pennsylvania dramatized the issue in opposing an appropriation of $3,665 for the mansion's upkeep. In what became famous as the "Gold Spoon Speech," he sarcastically described Van Buren as a "plain hard-handed democratic President [who uses] knives,

PRESIDENT LINCOLN, *tallest of the company, stands gravely with his guest Prince Napoléon, who wears a broad sash across his chest, while Secretary of State William H. Seward talks cheerfully of victory for the Union. Northerners showed special courtesy to the Prince, cousin of the Emperor of the French, and tried to hide their dismay at the course of the Civil War. The Lincolns gave this party in August, 1861, only two weeks after the Union defeat at Bull Run. In a flag-crowned pavilion, the Marine Band finishes its regular Saturday concert on the south lawn. Beyond a cluster of soldiers' tents rises the uncompleted Washington Monument.*

forks, and spoons of gold, that he may dine in the style of the monarchs of Europe."

Moreover, Ogle charged, the dapper President spent "the People's cash in . . . green finger cups, in which to wash his pretty tapering, soft, white lily fingers," and ate fancy French foods instead of good American " 'hog and hominy,' 'fried meat and gravy' . . . with a mug of 'hard cider.' "

Defenders quickly countered with documents showing that Van Buren had actually cost the taxpayers less for expenses than had any of his predecessors. It was too late. Too many voters were convinced that royally wicked living had gone on at the White House. William Henry Harrison, candidate of the Whig "Log Cabin and Hard Cider" Party, won the election handily.

For the next few years, no one could complain of too much White House festivity.

President Harrison, hero of the Indian battle on the Tippecanoe River, was the oldest man ever to achieve the Presidency. At 68, "Old Tippecanoe" felt fit enough to ride horseback to the Capitol where, coatless and hatless in icy wind, he delivered the longest inaugural oration in American history. Soon after, he developed a cold that turned into pneumonia. One month after taking office, he was dead.

Harrison's wife Anna never reached the Executive Mansion, the only First Lady to miss the experience. Unable to stand the rugged steamer and stagecoach trip at the time of the inaugural, she had been preparing to leave when a messenger rode up with the tragic news. Mrs. Harrison remained in the Ohio frontier country where her husband had made his name—and where their grandson, Benjamin Harrison, would eventually follow a similar career leading to the Presidency.

In the hushed East Room of the White House, on April 7, 1841, lay the body of

William Henry Harrison—the first President to die in office. The room was smothered in the "habiliments of woe" then deemed appropriate to such occasions. Two of the old General's swords glittered against the coffin's black velvet pall; his Bible and prayerbook rested on a nearby table.

Among the mourners sat the new President, John Tyler. The last half of the catchy campaign slogan, "Tippecanoe and Tyler Too," had become the first Vice President to move up to the top post as a result of his predecessor's death.

In his scant single term, President Tyler brought two First Ladies to the mansion.

His first wife, gentle Letitia, led the restricted life of an invalid on the second floor until her death in 1842.

She appeared in company only once. Wearing a simple dress and a soft lace cap that shaded her worn face and still-handsome dark eyes, she came downstairs for the marriage of the Tylers' third daughter, Elizabeth, to William Waller of Virginia.

"Lizzie has had quite a grand wedding," her sister-in-law, Mrs. Robert Tyler, wrote of the event. Dolley Madison was there, now 73 and as popular as ever. All official Washington attended, notably the eloquent Daniel Webster, then Secretary of State and a great friend of the family.

When someone remarked that the President's pretty daughter was giving up "belleship" to live in quiet Williamsburg, Webster quoted Sir Walter Scott.

"Love rules the court, the camp, the grove," he intoned in his deep voice, "and love is heaven and heaven is love."

Webster spoke more truly than he knew. In June, 1844, eight months before the end of his single term, the President would take a second wife in a private ceremony at New York City. The bride, vivacious young Julia Gardiner, had been something

HARPER'S WEEKLY, MARCH 15, 1902, COURTESY NEW-YORK HISTORICAL SOCIETY

SMITHSONIAN INSTITUTION

TO THE EMPEROR *and people of Germany and to Prince Henry of Prussia! Offering a toast, Theodore Roosevelt turns toward his guest of honor. At his left stands Sir Julian Pauncefote, the British Ambassador. Protocol had fretted the President—"Will the Prince take Mrs. Roosevelt [to dinner] while I walk in solemn state by myself? How do we do it anyhow?" His solution: a reception, with ladies; a dinner in the East Room, stag. Flags and eagles of the two nations brighten his menu for the Kaiser's brother.*

"YOU HAVE CLAIMED OUR HEART . . ." *President Johnson welcomes Britain's Princess Margaret and Lord Snowdon to the White House. In reply, she congratulated Mr. and Mrs. Johnson on their 31st wedding anniversary, November 17, 1965. In the East Room the Princess danced first with the President, then with her husband (below).*

of a belle herself during two social seasons in Washington.

In her brief but "auspicious reign," as she put it, Julia Tyler frankly delighted in the admiration and attention showered upon her. She received guests like a queen, seated on a raised platform in the Blue Room. Wearing a white satin ball gown, and a white headdress with diamonds and three ostrich feathers, she led the dancing in the East Room. She popularized the daring waltz and introduced a bouncy new Bohemian dance called the polka.

Writing her mother of one triumph, she said gleefully, "the British Minister, Pakenham, was there . . . and devoted to me. At least fifty members of Congress paid their respects to me, and all at one time."

The merry footsteps of Julia Tyler had hardly died away when strait-laced President and Mrs. Polk entered the White House. They promptly banned all dancing, cards, and such diversions. They gave dinner parties, but eliminated all refreshments from their grand receptions.

When a guest at one of these functions complimented the First Lady on the "genteel assemblage," Sarah Polk replied with

dignity, "Sir, I have never seen it otherwise."

Thus, with sunshine and frost, in good times and bad, the social seasons waxed and waned at the mansion. Even under the pressures of Civil War, official entertaining continued without letup.

There were dinners and receptions, with new Union generals and staff officers attending along with government officials, diplomats, and foreign visitors. And week after week the public levees went on.

At the Lincolns' first levee in March, 1861, people afoot and in carriages solidly jammed the streets and approaches.

Some were "in evening dress, others in morning suits," one guest recorded, "with gloves and without gloves; clean and dirty; all pressing in the same direction...." They crowded toward "the tall, rapidly bobbing head of the good 'Abe,' as he shook hands with his guests... when anyone he knew came along, he bent himself down to the necessary level, and seemed to whisper a few words in the ear, in pleasant, homely fashion."

Yet if Mary Lincoln arranged an elaborate party, critics complained she was heartlessly wasting money while brave boys died at the front. When she persuaded the President to substitute receptions for dinners, to save cash and greet more people, the cry arose that she was spending the money instead on the expensive finery that was known to be her weakness.

Whatever she did was wrong—this most maligned of First Ladies—yet the critical public committed acts of vandalism in her home that shocked all who saw them.

The White House looked "as if a regiment of rebel troops had been quartered there," observed a guard after Lincoln's second inaugural reception. The visitors had cut out souvenirs from brocaded window hangings and snipped floral designs from lace curtains. "How can they?" the President was heard to say in distress.

In the month of victory, April, 1865, Abraham Lincoln told of a strange dream. As he described it to his wife and an intimate friend, it seemed he was awakened in the night by "pitiful sobbing." Following the wails to the East Room, he found there a group of mourners gathered around a catafalque on which lay a figure in funeral garb, the face covered.

"The President," a soldier in the honor guard explained to the dreamer . . . "killed by an assassin."

WITHIN TWO WEEKS, Abraham Lincoln had been murdered by John Wilkes Booth, and his body lay on the catafalque in the East Room. Outside, thousands of mourners gathered, awaiting their turn to pass the bier. As the line coiled through the house, the sound of weeping filled the air.

During Reconstruction days, Andrew Johnson's womenfolk surprised Washington sophisticates by their natural charm and good taste in handling the responsibilities of executive entertaining.

"We are plain people from the mountains of Tennessee," said the Johnsons' married daughter, Martha Patterson, who took on the hostess chores for her ailing mother. "I trust too much will not be expected of us."

Then all the Johnsons proceeded to demonstrate how "plain people" could maintain cheerful dignity through the terrible period of the President's impeachment trial to his final vindication.

In a happier time, Mrs. Ulysses S. Grant found the White House "a garden spot of orchids . . . a constant feast of cleverness and wit, with men who were the brainiest . . . and women unrivalled for beauty, talent and tact."

The Grants held a lavish wedding in 1874 for their idolized daughter Nellie, not yet 19. The bridegroom, whom Nellie had met on a trip abroad, was Algernon Charles Frederick Sartoris, a nephew of the noted English actress Fanny Kemble.

The bride wore a white satin dress trimmed with the finest and most expensive Brussels point lace. The ceremony was performed under a huge floral wedding bell amid fashionably ornate furnishings, and followed by one of Grant's famous multi-course meals.

A New York reporter listed the wedding-breakfast menu in awe. It included soft-shelled crab, chicken croquettes, lamb cutlets, beef tongue in aspic, woodcock and snipe on toast, salad, seven kinds of dessert, and three beverages.

Miserable at the feast, however, was one participant—President Grant. Tears filled the eyes of the usually impassive father-of-the-bride.

Perhaps the most sedate gatherings ever held at the mansion were the mid-Victorian hymn sings and prayers to which President and Mrs. Rutherford B. Hayes asked close Congressional and Cabinet friends on Sunday evenings.

Even at state dinners, the Hayeses strictly enforced their rule against serving alcoholic beverages. The practice won national acclaim from teetotalers, and from at least one guest the dry remark that at such affairs "water flowed like wine." It also inflicted on Mrs. Hayes the unkind, undying nickname, "Lemonade Lucy."

Public interest in the personal and social life of the White House never reached a higher pitch than it did in 1886, when Grover Cleveland became the first President to marry under this roof.

"I want my marriage to be a quiet one," Mr. Cleveland had written after the news leaked out that he was engaged to beautiful young Frances Folsom, daughter of his former law partner. He might as well have asked Niagara Falls to stop flowing. The whole country buzzed with felicitations, curiosity—and gossip over the age disparity between the 49-year-old bachelor and his 21-year-old fiancée.

Newspapers detailed every movement of the couple. Orchestras played interminable

PRESIDENTIAL SCHOLAR *Susan Elizabeth Hochschild, a student at Oberlin College, talks with poet Marianne Moore and novelist John O'Hara in the Red Room. A recent high school graduate, she met them at a reception held June 8, 1965, for 121 winners of an award established "to encourage . . . intellectual attainment."*

NATIONAL GEOGRAPHIC PHOTOGRAPHER JOSEPH J. SCHERSCHEL

NATIONAL GEOGRAPHIC PHOTOGRAPHER JAMES P. BLAIR (RIGHT) AND ROBERT L. KNUDSEN

WHITE HOUSE FESTIVAL OF THE ARTS *offered "something . . . for the taste of everyone," said Mrs. Johnson, welcoming 400 guests on June 14, 1965. Above, Ivy Clear and Zelma Bustillo of the Robert Joffrey Ballet Company study Paul Manship's bronze "Dancer and Gazelles." Below, actress Helen Hayes and painter Peter Hurd stroll on the south lawn. At dinner, Mrs. Johnson sits between actor Gene Kelly (right) and photographer Edward Steichen. The program honored contemporary American achievement in the arts.*

THE WASHINGTON POST

wedding marches and the popular song from Gilbert and Sullivan's *Mikado*, "He's Going to Marry Yum-Yum."

The President himself planned the wedding to be as private as possible, yet worthy of his pride and joy in winning the captivating Miss Folsom. Fewer than 40 close friends and relatives received invitations, each handwritten by the bridegroom.

As the guests walked through the main floor's great reception hall into the state rooms, they found an extravaganza of flowers draped around marble columns, banked above mantels, massed in fireplaces, and entwined into initials "C.F."

Two five-foot candelabra from Andrew Jackson's time cast a soft glow over the Blue Room during the ceremony. The tall brown-haired bride wore no jewelry with her ivory satin dress that trailed a long train.

At the end of the ceremony, the Marine Band swept into the wedding march from *Lohengrin* while church bells all over town pealed out to the slow, booming accompaniment of the Navy Yard's 21-gun salute.

From that gala send-off, Frances Cleveland went on to win the Capital's heart. At her first public reception she cheerfully shook hands with an estimated 9,000 people. Confounding pessimists, she found exceptional happiness in her marriage.

"I can wish the women of our Country no greater blessing," she said, indignantly denying a campaign charge that her husband mistreated her, "than that their homes and lives may be as happy, and their husbands may be as kind, attentive, considerate and affectionate as mine."

Mrs. Cleveland and the household staff parted sadly in 1889, after the President's defeat. Saying goodbye to one member she asked him to take good care of things. "We're coming back just four years from today," she said. And so they did, when Cleveland was re-elected, the only man to hold two separate leases on this house.

From Theodore Roosevelt to Lyndon Johnson, 20th-century Presidents have enjoyed one great advantage over their predecessors—the separation of their executive offices from their home.

With funds voted by Congress in 1902, President Roosevelt built the West Wing extension, and made important structural improvements in the mansion itself.

The most notable changes in the house vastly increased the size of the cramped State Dining Room and restored the original sweep and simplicity to the East Room that had become cluttered with Victorian gilt and plaster.

At long last, Presidential families had the second floor all to themselves—with another floor for hospitality suitable to the host of an expanding world power.

Just as each new family in turn adopted the style of living dictated by its times and tastes, each has colored its social life with its own personality and regional flavor, as different as the Yankee reticence of Calvin Coolidge from the Old-West spirit of today's Texas tenants.

In March, 1965, President and Mrs. Johnson presented a program of American Indian dances, following a state dinner in honor of President and Mrs.

Maurice Yameogo, from Africa's young republic of Upper Volta.

On a temporary stage set up in the gold-draped East Ballroom, the performers swayed and whirled in ritual Indian dances to the traditional drumbeats and chants of their ancestors.

Teen-age students of modern America, these boys and girls had come from 14 tribes of the plains, the southwest, and the Pacific northwest. Their weird costumes, representing spirit gods and animals, were little different from those the early explorers of North America may have viewed with wonder upon confronting the first Americans for the first time.

"And to think," muttered someone in the darkened audience, "that they flew here for the show in a 707 jet!"

The incident points up the interweaving of past and present that is one of the charms of White House life.

"I give a feast to-day to Indian kings and aristocrats," President John Adams wrote on February 16, 1801.

From then on, many tribal leaders journeyed to Washington to attend the great white chief's national holiday celebrations.

In Jefferson's time, disgruntled European ministers felt, as one said, that "The President took care to show his preference for the Indian deputies on New Year's Day by giving us only a bow, while with them he entered into a long conversation."

Descendants of Indians of those early days still travel from distant states to take part in the pageantry of Presidential inaugurals. About 150 of them, some in feathers and buckskin, joined in President Johnson's 1965 parade. And in April, 1966, the President held a special ceremony in the East Room to swear in his new Commissioner for the Bureau of Indian Affairs. For the first time in 97 years this

NATIONAL GEOGRAPHIC PHOTOGRAPHERS JAMES P. BLAIR (RIGHT) AND JOSEPH J. SCHERSCHEL

official was an Indian—Robert L. Bennett, a member of the Oneida tribe of Wisconsin.

Looking back on the changing social scene at the White House, a perceptive student can discern a distinct pattern of characteristic interests and associations.

President "Teddy" Roosevelt emphasized the "strenuous life" he preached with bouts in the East Room by Japanese jujitsu experts and Chinese wrestlers.

The widely traveled Tafts entertained against a backdrop of Philippine furnishings brought from the lately acquired Islands where he had been the first American civil governor.

Woodrow Wilson, an idealistic intellectual, preferred quiet dinners with friends to the most dazzling state affairs. He refused to invite persons to the White House merely to further administration goals.

"I will not permit my home to be used," he said, "for political purposes."

After the tensions of World War I and the pall cast by Wilson's illness, genial Warren Harding and his wife Florence opened the mansion to friends and the public in what seemed the "normalcy" the President sought. Until Mr. Harding's heart attack and death in 1923, the round of private parties, formal functions, and lawn fêtes set records for festivity.

Then came Calvin Coolidge. Succeeding to the office from the Vice Presidency, "Silent Cal" struck the country's funnybone with his wry mannerisms. His granite reserve, combined with Grace Coolidge's warm friendliness, brought an engaging note of the unexpected to routine dinners and receptions.

The Capital chuckled most over the early-morning breakfasts to which the President invited Members of Congress from both political parties. "Eight o'clock is mighty early in Washington," Chief

EVERY CHRISTMAS *brings children to the mansion for parties all their own. At left, White House staff families watch couples swirling through the patterns of a Bavarian folk dance on December 23, 1965. And six days later, boys and girls of the diplomatic community heard the Old Guard Fife and Drum Corps. The Army musicians led them in a march to the State Dining Room for pink punch and cookies, and let them take turns blowing the shiny bugles.*

JAMES MONROE LAW LIBRARY (RIGHT) AND PAINTING BY NATIONAL GEOGRAPHIC ARTIST ROBERT C. MAGIS

Usher Ike Hoover later wrote of these meetings. "When the invitations were telephoned at the last moment . . . Democrats and Republicans both would start scratching their heads for excuses. Sickness in the family, even sickness of a friend, was a favorite. Some would ask, 'Are you sure the President means me?' "

Yet for all the jests, the Coolidges put up more house guests (exclusive of personal friends and relatives) than had any other First Family to date. One guest brought his horse. The horse, named Tony, arrived with western screen star Tom Mix to divert war veterans at a 1925 lawn party.

Under President and Mrs. Herbert Hoover, entertaining reached new proportions. This was due partly to increased postwar activity in government, and partly to the many friends the Quaker couple had made during years of relief work and war aid at home and abroad.

The Hoovers rarely dined alone, and often added last-minute guests. After ordering lunch for four one day, they ended with 40, their housekeeper recalled. The cook ransacked the refrigerator, and produced a miracle of croquettes, for which one consumer requested the recipe.

But certainly the longest and liveliest social era ever seen came in at a rush with the gregarious Franklin Roosevelt clan that would hold sway here from 1933 to 1945.

Despite her many other activities, Eleanor Roosevelt found time for a staggering number of official and personal luncheons, teas, dinners, and after-dinner programs.

In her book *This I Remember*, she gave totals for one year alone: 323 house guests, 4,729 served a meal, 14,056 offered light refreshments at teas and receptions.

More varied guests—from poets and playwrights to students, presidents, prime ministers, and nuclear scientists—came to the White House while the Roosevelts were there than during any other administration. More royalty called, too, though that record passed later to the Eisenhowers.

MARIA HESTER MONROE *(above), first President's daughter to be wed in the White House, married her cousin Samuel Lawrence Gouverneur on March 9, 1820. The family kept the ceremony private, but gave two evening receptions within a week. Then official and social leaders paid their "visits of congratulations" in the formal style of the time.*

CELEBRATING *his son's wedding, John Quincy Adams dances a lively Virginia Reel with the bride, the former Mary Catherine Hellen. John—the only White House bridegroom among Presidents' sons—talks with his mother at left. Beside the mirror at right stands the officiating clergyman, Dr. William Hawley, who had married the Gouverneurs eight years earlier. For details of this painting, researchers consulted government files on purchases for the "elliptical drawing room," the Blue Room of today.*

In a republic that likes a dash of regal spice in its democratic pudding, royal visitors have always stirred the most excitement. Often their presence highlighted the political and social life of the time.

As early as 1803, President Jefferson entertained Jérôme Bonaparte, Napoleon's youngest brother and future King of Westphalia, then seeking passage home in an American frigate. When the impetuous young man stayed on to marry the Baltimore belle, Betsy Patterson, the President gave a dinner for them.

The fast-growing Capital buzzed with excitement in 1841 over the arrival of the handsome young Prince de Joinville, son of Louis Philippe of France. President Tyler's dinner in his honor sparkled with the "Republican court's" diplomatic and military regalia in medals, gold braid, and swords. At the ball afterward, the Prince led the quadrille with the President's soon-to-be-married daughter, Elizabeth.

In the shadow of imminent civil war, in 1860, President James Buchanan took special pains to welcome England's Prince of Wales, later Edward VII.

It was the first time that an heir apparent to the British throne had visited the former colonies. On the crowded second floor of the mansion, the bachelor President (the only one who never married) gave up his own room to the Prince and slept on a sofa. Buchanan's niece and hostess, violet-eyed Harriet Lane, presided at a state banquet followed by fireworks on the lawn.

The evening went smoothly, thanks to Miss Lane's command of royal protocol, learned at Queen Victoria's court while her uncle had been American minister. But the same could not be said of the reception

FRANK LESLIE'S ILLUSTRATED

NEWSPAPER

No. 1,603.—Vol. LXII.] NEW YORK—FOR THE WEEK ENDING JUNE 12, 1886. [Price, 10 Cents. $4.00 Yearly. 13 Weeks, $1.00.

WASHINGTON, D. C.—THE WEDDING AT THE WHITE HOUSE, JUNE 2nd—THE MOTHER'S KISS.
From a Sketch by C. Bunnell.—See Page 261.

given to share the Prince with the public.

"The Royal party have certainly seen Democracy unshackled for once," reported a New York correspondent. "The rush at the doors was terrible. People clambered in and jumped out of the windows. . . ."

King David Kalakaua of the Sandwich Islands (now Hawaii) became the first ruling monarch to visit the White House. Invited by President Grant to a state dinner in 1874, the guest of honor sat with three of his retinue standing behind him. One carefully examined every dish before passing it to his sovereign.

Since World War I, an ever-lengthening procession of kings, queens, premiers, and presidents has walked between the pillars of 1600 Pennsylvania Avenue.

The King and Queen of the Belgians called on President Wilson in 1919, shortly after his incapacitating stroke.

Edith Wilson offered the visitors tea in the Red Room, then escorted them up to the President's bedroom. Lying in the great Lincoln bed, Wilson was having one of his better days. He seemed to enjoy the visit, and to appreciate their gift of a set of plates decorated with scenes of Belgium, where he had known his postwar triumph.

Both Presidents Wilson and Coolidge received another Prince of Wales—the pink-cheeked young man who was destined to inherit the British crown as Edward VIII, then renounce it for love, and step down to be Duke of Windsor.

Queen Marie of Rumania, however, made the biggest headlines of the Coolidge period. Entertained at a ceremonial dinner, the loquacious queen (her hair shingled

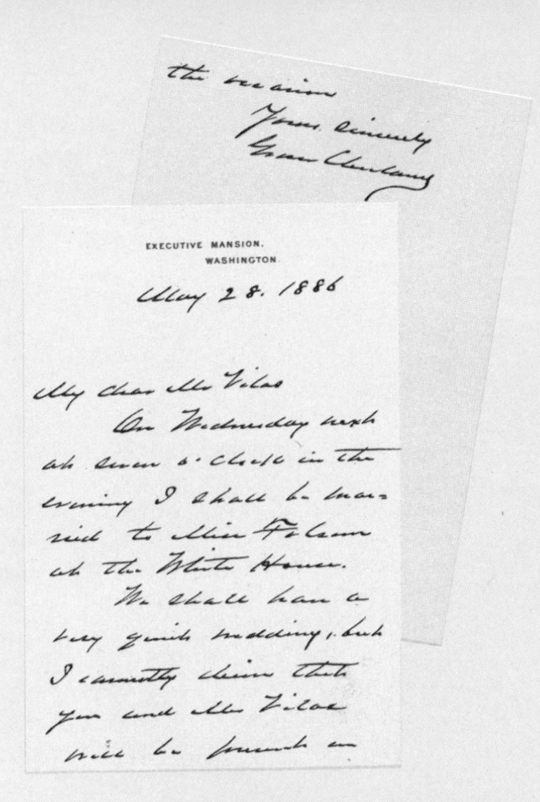

the occasion
Yours sincerely
Grover Cleveland

EXECUTIVE MANSION,
WASHINGTON.

May 28. 1886

My dear Mr Vilas
On Wednesday next at seven o'clock in the evening I shall be married to Miss Folsom at the White House.
We shall have a very quiet wedding, but I earnestly desire that you and Mrs Vilas will be present on

WISCONSIN STATE HISTORICAL SOCIETY (ABOVE) AND FRANK LESLIE'S ILLUSTRATED NEWSPAPER

GROVER CLEVELAND, *only President married in the White House, accepts a guest's congratulations as the ceremony ends. His bride, Frances, kisses her mother, Mrs. Oscar Folsom, widow of Cleveland's law partner. "Well might a President sue for her hand," reported* Leslie's, *"and a nation take pride in his choice."*

LIMITING HIS LIST *to family, close friends, and Cabinet officers, Cleveland wrote his own wedding invitations—the one above to the Postmaster General, William F. Vilas. Good wishes, old slippers, and rice rain down from the South Portico as the Clevelands leave the White House after a supper and cake-cutting in the private dining room.* Leslie's *gave full details of the bride's gray traveling costume and matching hat, commenting that she looked "very jaunty."*

and her dress short in the style of the twenties) made valiant efforts to engage the President in sociable table-talk.

"In this she was not any more successful," observed Chief Usher Ike Hoover, "than others who had tried it before."

The upheavals of World War II gave a new dimension to the hospitality of President and Mrs. Franklin Roosevelt. Beginning in 1938, German threats, then invasion, drove members of half a dozen royal houses of Europe to seek aid or refuge across the Atlantic. Some stayed at the Executive Mansion as house guests; others, like the Kings of Greece and Yugoslavia, passed through briefly. The Crown Prince and Princess of Norway spent Christmas holidays here in 1941. Queen Wilhelmina of the Netherlands visited in August, 1942.

British Prime Minister Winston Churchill came also—and often. The staff grew accustomed to seeing his roly-poly figure roaming the upstairs hall at night, poring over maps with President Roosevelt in the "strategy room," and dining with Churchillian gusto on whatever war-rationed items the domestic staff could scrape up.

Another important guest, Soviet Foreign Minister V. M. Molotov, remained several days in 1942. Reported as a mysterious "Mr. Brown," he urged the Allies to open a second front in Europe as soon as possible.

But the most famous visitors of the era were Britain's King George VI and Queen Elizabeth, who arrived in June, 1939, on the eve of war's outbreak. At one end of the broad central corridor along the family floor, the King occupied the Lincoln suite, the Queen the opposite Rose suite. Screens were set up to separate the Presidential and the royal areas.

Washington bruited about tales of protocol problems at such close quarters, of the search for a perfect blend of bottled water to make the royal tea, and of the insistence of the visiting servants on hot-water bottles and blankets for the royal entourage in the middle of a Washington heat wave.

"My lady likes to sleep warm," one maid explained to the Roosevelts' incredulous housekeeper, Mrs. Henrietta Nesbitt, who dutifully complied.

LIBRARY OF CONGRESS

Far more significant, the cordial relationship that developed then would strengthen British-American ties in the coming struggle. And this and similar friendships have continued to thrive.

After the war, two later generations of the Netherlands' royal family came in turn to the White House—Queen Juliana, and her daughter, Crown Princess Beatrix.

King George's stay with the Roosevelts had a sequel in President Truman's time, when young Princess Elizabeth brought her father's personal gift for the house, an 18th-century overmantel mirror. During the Eisenhower administration, she returned as Britain's reigning queen, Elizabeth II.

In November, 1965, President and Mrs. Johnson welcomed the Queen's younger sister, Princess Margaret, with her husband, the Earl of Snowdon, after their trip across the continent.

Before attending the White House dinner-dance held in their honor, the couple posed for news photographers under King George's mirror, now hanging in the Rose Guest Room where Princess Margaret's mother and sister had slept.

In the exchange of toasts following the dinner, the President addressed the Princess, radiant in pink dress and diamond jewels. "You have reminded us," he said, "that we are a young nation and a gay people who respond to the smile and the warmth of a young couple. . . . You have claimed our heart. . . ."

WORLD PROBLEMS, fast transport, and emerging nations have brought so many official visitors to Washington of late that the President's home can no longer accommodate them. Instead they usually occupy Blair House, the government's official guest residence across the street.

Nevertheless, White House entertaining goes on with new verve and imagination.

President and Mrs. Kennedy imbued state affairs with sophistication and artistic flair by inviting front-rank personalities in such fields as drama, ballet, and writing.

After a dinner given by the Kennedys

FOR WHITE HOUSE BRIDES: SILVER, SHEET MUSIC, AND SPOOFS

Admiring guests inspect the "exceedingly fine" presents sent to Nellie Grant on her marriage to Algernon Charles Frederick Sartoris. Leslie's *listed a "dessert set of eighty-four silver pieces," a "very handsome silver ice-cream service," a lace handkerchief "such as sell for $500," cameo and diamond rings, "an elegant Valenciennes lace fan," and "costly laces" from her father. When "Princess Alice" Roosevelt married Congressman Longworth of Ohio, the gifts were splendid—but not on display. Among the public tributes: a romantic new "national waltz," and a cartoonist's gentle jest.*

CARTOON FROM JUDGE (LEFT) AND COURTESY LESTER S. LEVY

in 1961 for Gen. Ibrahim Abboud of the Sudan, actors of the American Shakespeare Festival presented selections from several plays. On a stage set up in the East Room, one player spoke the familiar lines from the Prologue of *Henry V:*

> "A kingdom for a stage, princes to act
> And monarchs to behold the swelling scene."

"Quite a scene," remarked the director, "to play before a couple of presidents."

In another Kennedy innovation, little Caroline (aged 5) and John, Jr., (2) shared with 1,700 young guests from Washington child-care agencies the thrill of seeing a drill and dance by the Black Watch, Royal Highland Regiment. As a fall chill crept over the south lawn, it was hard to say which the children enjoyed more—the kilted men with their skirling bagpipes, or the cookies and gallons of hot chocolate.

Nine days later—with the shock of an assassin's bullet in Dallas, Texas—the Kennedy White House saga ended.

There remained only the epilogue: the flag-draped casket carried between the white columns in the pre-dawn mist of November 23, 1963, and the head-up courage of Jacqueline Kennedy, receiving the earth's great as they paid their last respects to the vibrant young man who had borne so many hopes.

In the East Room, the body of the slain President lay in state on a catafalque, as had that of President Lincoln a century before. At Mrs. Kennedy's request, black crape wreathed the chandeliers as at Lincoln's funeral. Again waves from a deed of senseless violence spread grief and horror across the country and the world.

But the Presidency never dies, whatever fate befalls its holders. In the plane that brought John Kennedy's body to Washington, Vice President Lyndon Baines John-

ROBERT L. KNUDSEN (BOTH)

WHIMSICAL FACE *smiles from the window at a buffet given by Luci Johnson for her wedding attendants three days before her marriage to Patrick Nugent on August 6, 1966. In the third-floor solarium, she leafs through photographs that trace her life from infancy. Lynda compiled the album as a gift for her sister and had it bound in Spanish leather. At right, Luci tries on her wedding gown before a Victorian dresser in the Lincoln Bedroom.*

son had taken the President's oath of office. Soon every American could be proud of the calm, efficient transfer of authority.

"By Monday night a transition was beginning to take place," reported Mrs. Johnson's press secretary, Elizabeth Carpenter. "We could feel the change in the questions the press asked—questions looking to the future."

As the working machinery of government turned, so did its social wheel. When White House entertaining resumed, it expressed the interests of a couple with a quarter-century of Congressional service and Capital friendships.

In 1965, for instance, the Johnsons gave ten informal buffet suppers for small groups of Congressmen and wives, instead of the traditional single reception. They also put on history's first Presidential cookout, moving charcoal broilers to the West Wing roof. The dinner menu—sizzling steaks, baked potatoes, corn pudding, and pecan pie—was as all-American as the guest list of retiring Members of Congress.

Still another "first" took a state dinner for West German Chancellor Ludwig Erhard outdoors to the Rose Garden. It was a perfect June evening. Japanese lanterns glowed over flower-decked tables, and the soaring Washington Monument and the Jefferson Memorial formed an enchanting backdrop no stage director could match.

One of the most spectacular gatherings sponsored by President and Mrs. Johnson spread from the building to the grounds, and lasted through the day and evening of June 14, 1965. Called the White House Festival of the Arts, it offered exhibits of contemporary American work in sculpture, painting, and photography, as well as a program of poetry and prose readings, drama, ballet, symphony and jazz.

Behind such varied events lies a fact of life, sometimes overlooked, in White House sociability. In official—or unofficial—entertaining, pleasure is often mixed with national purpose, from foreign policy and domestic aims to cultural expression.

The rule, however, has one large exception, the wedding of a President's daughter.

There is a story-book romance about such occasions that comes, perhaps, from association with princesses in enchanted castles. So far seven daughters have been married in Washington while their fathers held the highest office. Six selected the White House as the setting for both the ceremony and reception.

The latest bride, President Johnson's younger daughter Luci, set her wedding at the National Shrine of the Immaculate Conception on August 6, 1966. A recent convert to the Roman Catholic faith, she had often worshiped there with her fiancé, Patrick John Nugent of Waukegan, Illinois.

The bride's parents held the wedding reception at the Executive Mansion, adorned with floral arrangements dominated by the bridal color theme of pink and white.

NATIONAL GEOGRAPHIC PHOTOGRAPHERS DEAN CONGER AND JAMES P. BLAIR

JOINING HANDS, *Luci and Patrick Nugent begin cutting the first slice from their tiered eight-foot wedding cake. A moment later, the President stepped forward to help when the icing resisted the silver knife. Lynda, the maid of honor, dances with the bridegroom among family friends gathered in the East Room (below).*

NATIONAL GEOGRAPHIC PHOTOGRAPHER DEAN CONGER

"It's been a beautiful, wonderful day," said 19-year-old Luci Nugent, as she and her handsome blond husband finally waved goodbye to the wedding party and guests assembled on the south lawn. It was also a day marked by the paradox of change, yet continuity, that goes with living in this historic house.

As in any bride's home, preparation had begun early. But with a difference: The chattering young bridesmaids dressed in the Lincoln Room, with its massive Victorian furniture. On one wall hung their pink moiré dresses. And across the Lincoln bed stretched the bride's long white veil, carefully arranged to avoid wrinkles.

In spite of the solemnity of the Nuptial Mass and the social pageantry of the reception, the "personal and sentimental" spirit that Mrs. Johnson had sought came through clearly. It showed, for instance, in the young couple's happy tears at the altar, and in the warm embraces exchanged by President and Mrs. Johnson with old friends passing along the receiving line in the East Room.

FRANK WOLFE (RIGHT) AND ROBERT L. KNUDSEN

Never before had the public seen so much of a White House marriage. Long-range cameras hidden in the church recorded every detail; television equipment massed on the mansion's south lawn and set up briefly in the state rooms flashed scenes nationwide to fifty million viewers.

More than half a century had passed since the last Washington wedding of a President's daughter. Then Woodrow Wilson gave away two within six months—Eleanor in the spring of 1914, and Jessie the previous fall.

Because of her mother's illness, Eleanor Wilson's marriage to Secretary of the Treasury William Gibbs McAdoo was kept a small and quiet affair. But no such shadow limited the gaiety and brilliance of the earlier nuptials uniting her sister with law professor Francis B. Sayre.

The *Washington Post* told readers, in banner headlines and florid phrases of the day: "NATIONS OF ALL THE WORLD DO HOMAGE TO WHITE HOUSE BRIDE AS SHE TAKES SOLEMN VOWS AMID SCENES OF UNEQUALED SPLENDOR"

Even more excitement had surrounded the 1906 wedding of Theodore Roosevelt's daughter Alice to Congressman Nicholas Longworth of Ohio.

Drama and glamour touched everything connected with this high-spirited daughter of the popular, exuberant President. Her marriage and reception, attended by a thousand guests, became the talk of national and international society. Her gifts ranged from a chest of silks given by the Empress Dowager of China to a hogshead of popcorn sent by a dealer; from a pearl necklace from the Republic of Cuba to a feather duster and a box of snakes.

To Alice Roosevelt's wedding came Nellie Grant Sartoris, White House bride of 32 years before. In turn, Mrs. Longworth attended Luci Johnson's wedding, 60 years after her own.

Thus another chain of continuity in this house—the story of love and the celebration of marriage—now reaches unbroken across nearly a century.

FROM THE SOUTH PORTICO, *the bride tosses her bouquet of lilies-of-the-valley to her sister Lynda. Then a poignant moment follows the lighthearted one—Mr. and Mrs. Nugent say goodbye to Mr. and Mrs. Johnson before leaving the nation's first home.*

III The

Family at Home

BEHIND THE GLITTERING CURTAIN of political power and social prestige, Presidential families have tried, with varying success, to carry on normal personal lives. This has not been easy, though there are compensations.

How many wives, for instance, could have an experience such as this one that Mrs. Johnson relates?

"All our married life," she said, "my gregarious husband has brought home unexpected guests. One day he phoned that he had invited two friends for lunch, not mentioning their names. We had hash that day, and our guests turned out to be former President Truman and the great Texas historian, J. Frank Dobie. If our food was rather low-flown, the conversation more than made up for it!"

Every First Lady has faced the special problems that go with her position. The public takes a personal interest in the way she runs her home, or dresses, or does her hair, as they would not think of doing in the case of a private individual.

Mrs. Hoover once received a letter from a visitor taking her to task because a curtain in one of the public rooms had been darned rather than replaced. The President's wife, said Eleanor Roosevelt, comes to feel that she is not clothing herself, "but dressing a national monument."

Most frustrating of all, affairs of state often leave a Chief Executive with little or no time for his wife and children.

". . . I doubt if the public realizes," Mrs. Roosevelt wrote in her memoirs, "the price that the whole family pays in curtailment of opportunity to live a close family life."

INAUGURATION DAY *begins like many other days—the President breakfasts in his bedroom, the First Lady stops in for a quiet moment. But on this occasion, January 20, 1965, they share a historic schedule: the ceremony at the Capitol, the parade past the White House, the inaugural balls. "I was probably saying, 'Hurry up, Lyndon,'" Mrs. Johnson recalls with a smile.*

Yet each executive family, in its own way, has made the necessary adjustment to the country's larger interests. Most have managed to relax and be themselves amidst the trials and privileges of their position.

There was more leisure, of course, in the early days of the Republic. President Jefferson found great satisfaction in his many diversions, from horseback riding to experimenting with plants that he hoped might prove helpful in developing the young nation's agriculture. He read voraciously. His personal library, which he eventually sold to the government, contained some 6,500 volumes.

As a widower who had lost his wife Martha 20 years before, Jefferson welcomed visits from his married daughters, Martha Randolph and Maria Eppes. During Mrs. Randolph's stay in the winter of 1805 and 1806, her eighth child, James Madison Randolph, became the first baby born in the White House.

A fond grandfather, the President enjoyed playing with his daughters' active broods. When the great German naturalist,

AFTERNOON AT HOME: *Mrs. Johnson serves tea in the West Sitting Hall to a group of ambassadors' wives, supplementing the large receptions for the growing number of diplomats in Washington today. On the wall hangs Mary Cassatt's "Mother and Two Children," acquired for the White House in 1966. In the nation's early years, a President's wife could entertain all the ladies of the diplomatic circle at gatherings little larger than this. The second-floor hall in Mrs. Benjamin Harrison's time included a staircase, removed in 1902.*

DISTRICT OF COLUMBIA PUBLIC LIBRARY

Baron von Humboldt, visited Jefferson in 1804, he found him romping on the floor with his grandchildren.

"You have found me playing the fool, Baron," he greeted this friend with whom he shared many scientific interests, "but I am sure to *you* I need make no apology."

John Quincy and Louisa Adams, whose three boys were grown when the family came to the mansion, followed Jefferson's example of experimental plantings. The President was especially interested in mulberry trees for silkworm culture. He once wrote that Mrs. Adams was "winding silk from several hundred silkworms that she has been rearing. . . ."

Adams liked an occasional game of billiards in the evening, for which he was criticized as a "corrupter of youth." But no one could carp at his sterner recreations, duly recorded in his diary.

He usually rose "from an hour and a half to two hours before the sun." Then, depending on the season, he would take a four-mile walk or a swim in the nearby Potomac before returning for the day's work.

Out of Adams's morning dip came one of the best yarns of White House folklore. It concerned a woman journalist named Anne Royall, who was famous for her enterprise in ferreting out news. Having failed to obtain an interview with the President

WITH DEEP CONCERN, *but inadequate medical resources, physicians wait with Mrs. Garfield as the President struggles to recover from an assassin's wound. Through the long July days of 1881, an improvised cooling system—with 31 tons of ice and 3,000 feet of toweling—kept the temperature near 70° in the second-floor sickroom. Dr. Susan Edson, who nursed the patient, holds a palm-leaf fan sent by a Philadelphia firm. By special permission, a newspaper artist sketched scenes of the long vigil. Hope vied with anxiety in each day's public bulletins until the President died in September.*

on the controversial issue of the Bank of the United States, she tracked him down to his favorite spot along the river bank. There, the story goes, she sat on his clothes while he remained submerged to his neck, until he had answered her questions.

Like many other harried executives, Presidents have often relaxed with sports. President Grant, who had been a daring horseman since his youth, liked to drive a fast horse-and-buggy. He was once stopped by a Washington policeman for exceeding the carriage speed limit. When the officer discovered the culprit's identity, he hesitated to issue the ticket. Grant, however, directed him to do his duty, and paid the $20 collateral for the offense.

Theodore Roosevelt enjoyed vigorous exercise. While Chief Executive, he helped tame the brutal game of football by calling a White House conference that led to new rules for the protection of players.

President Taft tossed out the first baseball of the 1910 season, thus inaugurating a custom still followed. Golf was a favorite diversion of Presidents Harding and Eisenhower—30 years apart. Herbert Hoover, long an expert and ardent fisherman, continued the tranquil pastime at his Virginia summer camp as a respite from the grim problems of the depression.

On the other hand, perhaps no man ever arrived at the White House with less interest in sports than Calvin Coolidge. His friend and Secret Service agent, Edmund Starling, told of initiating the President into the arts of fishing and clay-pigeon shooting. Colonel Starling also persuaded his boss to exercise in his bedroom on an electric horse someone had sent him. ". . . we rode every day," Starling recalled, "playing cowboy like a couple of kids."

From Franklin Roosevelt on, all Presidents (and quite a few staff members) have enjoyed swimming in the indoor pool presented to the polio-crippled President in 1933 by a sympathetic public. To F.D.R., as to John Kennedy, who suffered from a back injury, this pool offered an aid to health as well as all-important recreation.

President Roosevelt also found release from care in the intricacies of stamp collecting. And President Kennedy, who read avidly and deeply, might momentarily sink real world problems in the outrageous adventures of spy thrillers.

Bringing the score up to date, President Johnson relaxes by riding and hunting at his ranch under the big Texas sky. And, when pressures have permitted, no Chief Executive since George Washington has shown more zest for dancing. Washington stepped to the minuet and swung his partner in the Virginia Reel. President Johnson added dancing to the ultraformal

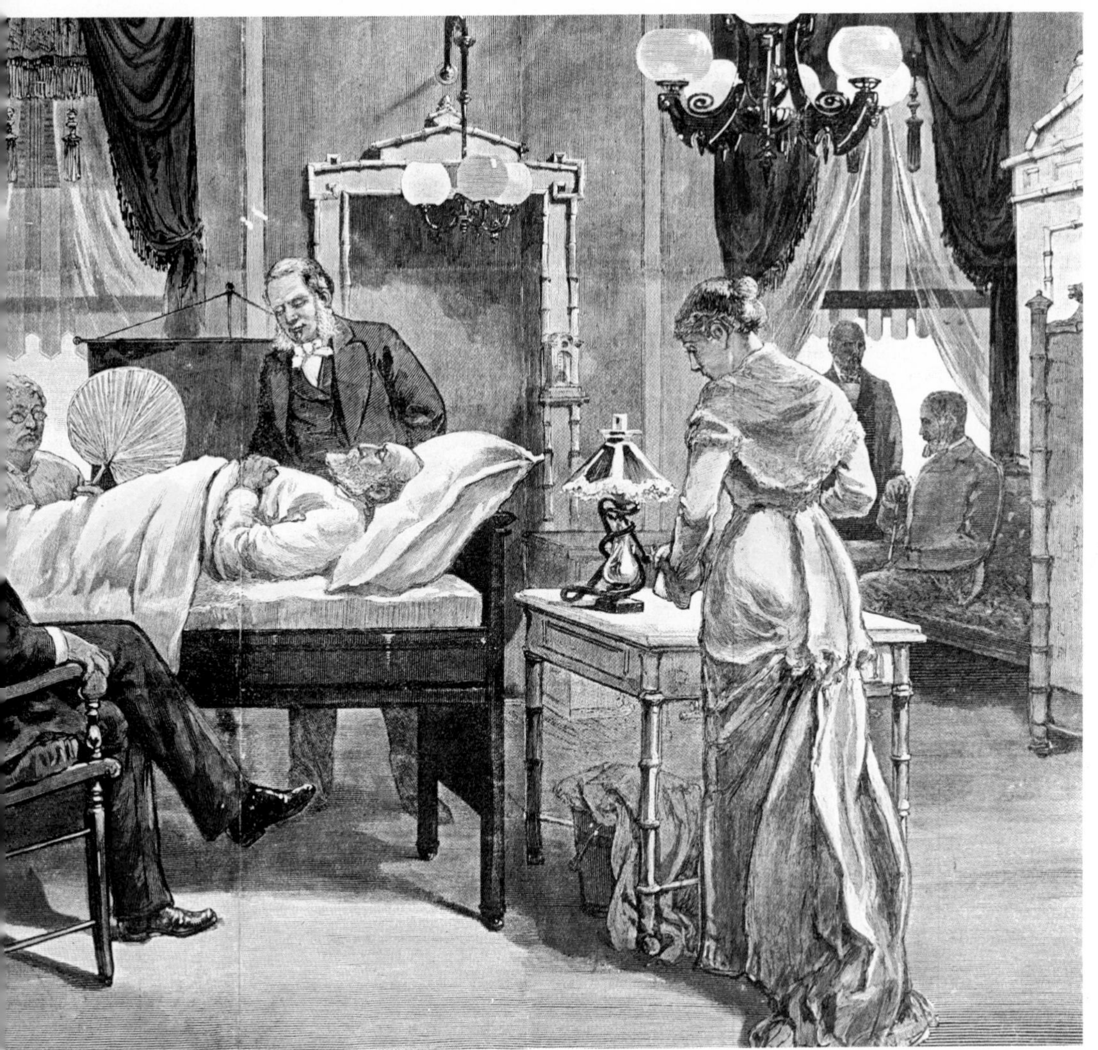

KIPLINGER COLLECTION

diplomatic receptions, and, on one occasion, at least, waltzed some 50 guests in turn around the East Room floor.

On the domestic side, First Ladies have always faced formidable problems in keeping house at the administrative heart of the nation. From the early 19th century until 1902, the President's family had to share the limited space of the mansion's second floor with the executive staff.

Up and down the public stairway, and sometimes along the private corridor, tramped callers of all kinds, including solicitors, job hunters, and tradesmen, as well as Cabinet officers and ambassadors. As late as 1881, according to a member of President Garfield's staff, a mere acquaintance "pushed himself in past the doors that marked the private domain . . . and took his afternoon siesta upon the most comfortable sofa he could find."

With the main floor also partly open to the public, some of the older and frailer wives seldom left their second-floor quarters. From her bedroom the first Mrs. Tyler regulated all household affairs, and "so quietly," her devoted daughter-in-law wrote her own family, "that you can't tell when she does it. All the clothes for the children, and for the servants, are cut out under her immediate eye. . . . All the cake, jellies, custards, and we indulge largely in them, emanate from her, yet you see no confusion. . . ."

By preference, Mrs. Zachary Taylor—another dedicated homemaker—left the arrangements for official entertaining to her attractive married daughter, Betty Bliss. She devoted her attention to her family, her close friends, and visiting Southern relatives who arrived in droves and stayed for weeks, in the old-fashioned way.

FRED WARD, BLACK STAR

FROM THE BALCONY *that President Truman added to the South Portico, Caroline Kennedy and John, Jr., watched fascinating events of state on the lawn. Their English nannie, Miss Maud Shaw, once told Mr. Truman how much they enjoyed the balcony; recalling the controversy when it was built in 1947, he said with a twinkle that he was glad someone liked it.*

Margaret Taylor had dreaded her husband's Presidential prospects. He deserved retirement, she felt, after 40 years of active military service in the War of 1812, frontier skirmishes with Indians, and the Mexican War. She prayed nightly for his defeat, General Taylor told amused friends who wanted him nominated in 1848. His success, she declared, would shorten his life.

Barely 16 months after Taylor's inaugural, her gloomy prophecy came true.

On July 4, 1850, the President sat under a blazing sun at an Independence Day celebration on the grounds of the unfinished Washington Monument. Returning to the White House, he became ill of what was then called cholera morbus—the result, according to legend, of his having consumed quantities of iced milk and raw cherries. In five days he was dead, and handsome, robust Vice President Millard Fillmore had succeeded to the highest office.

After his own term had expired, Fillmore remarked that when he learned of the tragedy, and thought of the great responsibilities he would face, he spent "the only sleepless night he ever passed on account of political anxiety."

Yet in shadowed or happy times, every President arrives at the Executive Mansion with fresh hopes and ambitions. As in any other new home, each First Lady arranges the family possessions, and makes her own household changes. Former schoolmistress Abigail Fillmore, who had met ambitious young Millard as his teacher, was dismayed to find that the government had supplied no reference books for executive use.

The President persuaded Congress to appropriate funds to establish the first official library, and immediately ordered a dictionary, a Bible, and a national atlas. As other books arrived, she arranged them in mahogany cases in the upstairs oval sitting room. And here the Fillmores spent many evenings quietly reading, or listening to their talented daughter Mary Abigail, who played the piano, harp, and guitar.

THE MOST PERSONAL PART of the house has always been the second-floor suite stretching west of the centered oval chamber. Made up of about eight rooms, it serves as a sanctuary for the President and his family.

Here, in 1868, gentle Eliza Johnson rocked and sewed as she awaited the verdict in her husband's nightmarish impeachment trial at the Capitol. "I knew he would be acquitted," she told the messenger through happy tears. "I knew it."

In Eleanor Roosevelt's study, Vice President Truman heard from her the news of President Roosevelt's death. "Is there anything I can do for you?" he asked Mrs. Roosevelt. "Is there anything *we* can do for *you?*" she replied. "For you are the one in trouble now."

Through the years, the executive apartment has reflected the nation's changing taste in home decor—from the fine, handcrafted pieces of the Federal period to the fuss and plush of Victorians, and the functional designs of the mid-20th century.

With each new tenant came individual belongings that hinted at their owner's way of life. Jefferson's flair for gadgets (he called them "conveniences") showed up in a mechanical device he installed in his large wardrobe. A kind of turnstile, it

JAMES K. W. ATHERTON, UNITED PRESS INTERNATIONAL

MAJESTIC COLUMNS *of the South Portico frame Mrs. Dwight D. Eisenhower on the balcony as she waves a birthday greeting to her husband, 70 years old on October 14, 1960.*

revolved to bring forward whatever garment he wanted.

President and Mrs. William McKinley, for instance, moved in with their knickknacks and fancy cushions and settled down among the curlicued, tufted furniture that typified the 1890's.

In their big northwest bedroom, semi-invalid Ida whiled away the hours crocheting cozy slippers. Out of the yarn continually unwinding from her ever-present crochet bag, she made hundreds of blue "comfies" for friends, relatives, and charity.

Even the passing color schemes in the family apartment told something of the personalities of its various First Ladies.

Blithe Dolley Madison made lavish use of vivid yellow decor. Sedate Mrs. Hayes had her bedroom walls "tinted pale blue, with panels of light gray and pink," wrote a woman correspondent of the 1870's. Mrs. Eisenhower, who liked fluffy, feminine accessories, chose "Mamie pink," as it came to be known in fashion circles, for the dominant shade in her redecoration.

Like Dolley Madison, Mrs. Lyndon Johnson has shown a strong preference for yellow. Her favorite room, she often says, is the upstairs Yellow Oval Room, with its view of the Washington Monument. This sunny color, carried over from the Kennedy period, still brightens the walls, draperies, and upholstery of a chamber used both as a family sitting room and as a more private area to receive formal guests.

Outside, in the broad transverse corridor, with its additional sitting-room space, off-white walls give the historic floor a modern look. Moreover, these walls, like the plain yellow surfaces, offer a perfect background to display the priceless paintings lately acquired by Mrs. Kennedy and Mrs. Johnson, acting in turn with respective art committees to add to the permanent White House collection.

But it was a President, not a First Lady,

NATIONAL GEOGRAPHIC PHOTOGRAPHER JAMES P. BLAIR

"**IT MEANS SO MUCH** *to me to have young people stay at the White House," says Mrs. Johnson, "where you always feel close to the great events of our history. We want to share this house with citizens of the future, and so we invite them whenever we can." At left, the President pauses for a word with Lynda, Miss Mary Rather, his secretary in Congressional days, her niece Nancy, and other Texas guests. Above, the First Lady refills plates at a picnic lunch.*

EXCHANGING GIFTS *with their guest, the Johnsons welcome India's Prime Minister Indira Gandhi (right) in the Yellow Oval Room. First woman to visit the White House as an elected head of government, she brought a ceremonial saddle, books on Indian art, and brilliant saris.*

WHITE TIGER *at the White House: Mr. Eisenhower gets a close look at Mohini, presented to him by broadcasting executive John Werner Kluge as a gift to the children of the United States. Reared in India, she now lives at the National Zoological Park in Washington.*

THE PEOPLE *share a Presidential treat (opposite): Andrew Jackson received a 1,400-pound cheese from a New York dairy farmer and served it at his last public levee in 1837. Some ate it on the spot "without crackers," according to an eyewitness who found it "excellent."*

THOMAS J. ABERCROMBIE © N.G.S. (BELOW) AND SMITHSONIAN INSTITUTION

ORNATE DIAMOND BROOCH *from the Sultan of Turkey, sent to Benjamin Harrison, honors the 400th anniversary of Columbus's discovery of America. The President accepted it for the nation and sent it to the State Department. The Smithsonian Institution displays it now.*

NATIONAL GEOGRAPHIC PHOTOGRAPHER JAMES P. BLAIR (ABOVE) AND PERLEY'S REMINISCENCES

who made the cleanest sweep of all in altering the mansion's interior decoration.

Chester A. Arthur, on taking over as Chief Executive in 1881 after Garfield's death, said he would not live in a house that looked like this one. Nor did he.

After moving into a borrowed residence, he collected 24 wagonloads of old and battered furniture, rugs, and ornaments from the basement to the attic of the White House. Among the discards was the rat trap, commented an irreverent reporter, that caught the rat that ate the suit that belonged to Mr. Lincoln.

He sold the lot at public auction, and substituted new furnishings throughout, including state rooms elaborately redone in the gilt, silver, and velvet then considered the height of elegance.

To provide more privacy and keep out the drafts that had long circulated freely, Arthur also had a floor-to-ceiling translucent wall built across the back of the main reception hall. Designed with flags and eagles "interlaced in the Arabian method," it was the marvel and delight of visitors.

Amid such shifting scenes, the very human men and women who passed this way have known the trials and errors, pleasures and miseries, that come to all of us.

Wealthy, fastidious Arthur lived luxuriously in the White House. Yet behind the fashionable façade, he was the affectionate father of a 9-year-old daughter and a college-age son, and a lonely widower who had lost his wife Ellen only the year before he came to office. Every day he had fresh flowers placed by Ellen's photograph.

The ritual recalls another act of devotion half a century earlier. In his bedroom each night, the crusty old warrior Andrew Jackson would slip off the precious miniature of his wife Rachel, worn close to his heart. He would set it up on the table where he could see her face in the morning, next to her old, worn Bible.

Jackson's daily life, however, had its consolations. He filled the house with visiting nieces and nephews from Tennessee, who came often and brought their children.

Rachel's nephew, Andrew Jackson Donelson, made his home with the President as

STAND UP FOR SISTER: *Caroline Kennedy tries to lift her little brother John, who remains as relaxed as the toys propped on her pink-and-white bed—her favorite doll, "Raggedy-Annie," and her stuffed poodle "Tinkerbelle."*

FOR THE ADULTS *of any First Family, hours of conversation come all too rarely. Here, Mrs. Johnson joins her daughters in Luci's bedroom to hear Lynda's account of her vacation trip through the west in the summer of 1965, and to see the photographs she brought home.*

his private secretary. Donelson's winsome, delicate wife Emily served as official hostess, and here were born three of their four children, two girls and a second boy.

Fair-haired Mary Rachel, first of these White House babies, was the apple of Uncle Andrew's eye. Many years later, she looked back on those happy days and recalled tenderly how Jackson indulged the little ones: "Always serving the children first, saying they have better appetites, less patience, and should not be required to wait. . . ."

After struggling with the grim issues of his stormy administration, President Jackson relaxed in carefree frolics with the small members of his large household. He joined them in their playroom, and often got up early to go outdoors with them for a game of "mumble-the-peg."

From the beginning, children of all ages, toddlers to teens, have loved the big house — its fascinating nooks and corners, its feeling of mysterious, important happenings.

Most of the very young ones have been grandchildren, since the top political prize has gone usually to men well along in years.

In 1800, John and Abigail Adams brought to the mansion its first child, their four-year-old granddaughter who lived with them for the rest of their lives. Little Susanna promptly came down with whooping cough. But she lived to become a grandmother herself, and to tell *her* Susanna of this and happier experiences in the bleak, incomplete house by the Potomac.

The most famous grandchild of his time was undoubtedly "Baby McKee," who lived with his grandparents, parents, cousins, aunt, uncle, and great-grandfather in Benjamin Harrison's big household of the early 1890's.

Popular and news photography was just then coming in, and amateurs and professionals haunted the grounds hoping to get a shot of Benjamin "Baby" McKee, perhaps taking a walk with his grandfather,

CULVER SERVICE

HARPER'S BAZAR (SIC) 1896 (ABOVE) AND DRAWING BY F. W. BROUARD

CRACKLING FIRE *warms Mrs. Cleveland during a quiet hour. At her desk beside the window, she wrote to relatives and friends after getting the children ready for their day's activities. The portrait has been published as one of Mrs. Cleveland and baby Marion, now Mrs. John Harlan Amen, but Mrs. Amen believes it may show her sister Esther, born in the White House in 1893.*

ALGONQUIN, *"the most absolute pet of them all," as T.R. said, clatters in to visit Archie Roosevelt, in bed with measles. Quentin, youngest of the boys, coaxed the pony into the elevator with the help of a White House coachman. Kermit leads the small parade into Archie's second-floor bedroom.*

UNITED PRESS INTERNATIONAL

IN HONOR *of the first President, Mrs. Herbert Hoover plants a young cedar near the tennis courts on the south lawn, during a simple ceremony on March 23, 1932. The tree came from George Washington's boyhood home, Ferry Farm, near Fredericksburg, Virginia.*

"**TO WORK** *for a more beautiful America," says the First Lady, "is—in the words of our oldest declaration—to assist in the pursuit of happiness." Here, in the Treaty Room, Mrs. Johnson confers with members of her committee on beautification of the national Capital.*

or riding in his own little goat-drawn cart.

The goat, called "His Whiskers" by the coachman, provided the press with its best story concerning the much-publicized boy. Hitched to his red cart bearing Baby McKee, His Whiskers once ran away down the driveway and into Pennsylvania Avenue, with the stout President in frock coat and top hat close behind in furious pursuit.

Only one President's child has been born in the White House. Esther Cleveland, the second daughter of Grover and Frances Cleveland, came into the world in her mother's upstairs bedroom.

The event occurred in 1893, six months after Esther's father began his second term. Her sister Ruth was nearly two years old then, and before the President left office, another sister, named Marion, was born at their summer home in Massachusetts.

The three pretty and charming little girls were "much beloved by everyone around the place," Chief Usher Ike Hoover recalled in his memoirs of four decades at the White House. People all over the country sent them toys and garments, and wrote letters of advice on their upbringing.

When Ruth first arrived, curious Washingtonians gathered on the lawn to watch the infant and her nurse at their daily airings. Cooing women sometimes picked her up and passed her from one to another with pats and kisses.

Mrs. Cleveland had to order the gates to the south lawn closed to the public—an action that led to false and cruel rumors that Ruth was abnormal.

More than 60 years would pass before

NATIONAL GEOGRAPHIC PHOTOGRAPHER JAMES P. BLAIR

another President's infant, John Kennedy, Jr., came here to live. Two-month-old "John-John," as the nation knew him, and his three-year-old sister Caroline found a different world from that of the Cleveland girls. But public interest in the latest youngsters burned as brightly as ever.

No detail was too insignificant to report, including the children's first snowman on the lawn, the jungle gym behind the shrubbery, or their third-floor playroom, where the Eisenhower grandchildren had romped before them.

John Junior's and Caroline's adventures with the important grown-ups they encountered have gone down in the never-ending juvenile history of this house: How John, aged two, refused to greet the Grand Duchess of Luxembourg because no one had given him his usual fortification of a cookie and ginger ale. How Caroline, a child of the space age, met and talked with astronauts. "Where's the monkey?" she asked John Glenn, after his pioneering flight which had followed the experimental orbits of chimpanzees.

But the two White House generations shared at least one common childhood experience. Both Mrs. Cleveland and Mrs. Kennedy established here a kindergarten attended by their own children and a small group of young friends.

Other children of other Presidents have left behind memories of a different sort—memories of sadness and of carefree pranks that evoke long-past eras.

With Abraham and Mary Lincoln came Tad, not quite eight, Willie, going on 11, and 17-year-old Robert, usually away at college. The Lincolns were indulgent parents who often said, "Let the children have a good time." And this they surely did—especially mischievous Tad, who had the warm nature and quick temper of his mother, and Willie, gentle and thoughtful like his father. Together, they carried on highjinks that the President thoroughly enjoyed, and from time to time would join in, as when they all tumbled about the floor in a wrestling match.

BESET by the responsibilities and miseries of the Civil War, Lincoln often turned for relief to Tad's comic escapades. He quickly forgave the lad for such capers as eating the strawberries that had been ripened early for a state dinner, and using his toy cannon to bombard the door leading to a Cabinet meeting.

Lincoln had almost as much fun with the boys' pet dogs, ponies, and goats as they did. He liked to watch the goats jump about the lawn, and when one disappeared, he wrote a sad letter telling how "poor Nanny" had last been seen "chewing her little cud, on the middle of Tad's bed."

President and Mrs. Lincoln took pleasure and pride in Willie's literary bent, shown in his writing of short speeches and verse. It was a shattering blow when Willie suddenly became ill of a fever in February, 1862, and died soon after.

The President, a bit more stooped and somber, bore both his grief and the nation's burdens. Mary Lincoln, however, could not be reconciled to her loss. In the frantic hope of receiving a "message" from her beloved son, she arranged a spiritualist session at the Soldiers' Home—the Lincolns' "summer White House"—with a medium whose services were much in demand by families who had lost husbands, sons, and brothers in the war.

For a time Mrs. Lincoln believed that Willie had returned to her, telling her sister, "He comes to me every night and stands at the foot of my bed, with the same sweet, adorable smile he always had." Later she wrote, ". . . the loved & idolized being, comes no more."

There are stories that Lincoln himself attended at least one seance, though it is not clear whether he did so to humor his wife, check on the medium's tricks, or to satisfy curiosity born of his own streak of mysticism. One account has it that the President joked about the conflicting suggestions offered by "Napoleon," "Lafayette," and other spirits on the conduct of the war.

"Their talk and advice," he said, "sound very much like the talk of my Cabinet."

Among the happiest and closest families to live in the White House was that of Ulysses and Julia Grant. In a book of reminiscences written many years later, their youngest son Jesse described himself then as "an ordinary freckle-faced small boy . . . who adored his father and mother, his two brothers and sister, and was in turn much loved and petted by them."

After viewing the cramped living quarters and damp basement kitchen of their new home, Mrs. Grant would have preferred to stay in her comfortable Washington home, and use the Executive Mansion only for entertaining. But 11-year-old Jesse was delighted with the move.

There was the stable, with its gleaming carriage and harness, where Albert the coachman tended the President's Thoroughbred horses and Jesse's pony Reb. From the mansion's rooftop at night, the youngster studied the heavens through a fine gift telescope. With neighborhood pals, he formed a baseball club that grew

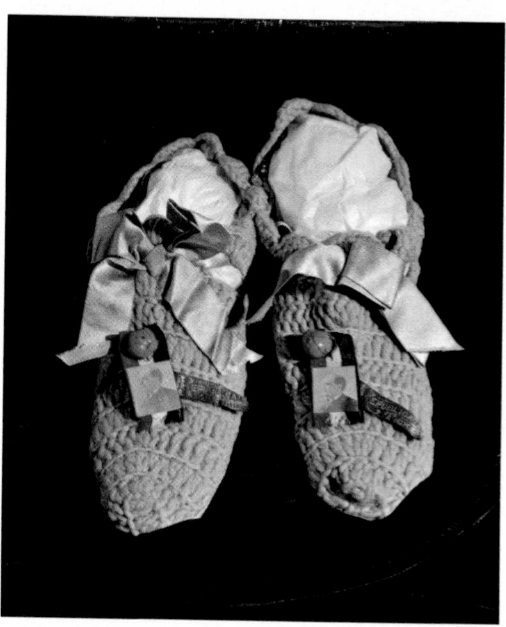

SMITHSONIAN INSTITUTION

CROCHETED SLIPPERS, *the handiwork of Mrs. William McKinley, carry a campaign appeal and photographs of her husband. The First Lady fashioned scores of similar "comfies" for charities and for children and friends.*

LIBRARY OF CONGRESS

TAKING SPECIAL DELIGHT *in such fragrant flowers as hyacinths and roses, the McKinleys kept the White House filled with bouquets. In their room (above), the First Lady placed vases of flowers and, above her husband's photograph, a string of horseshoes for luck. Despite uncertain health, she entertained as often as she could, decorating the state rooms with floral pieces in the shape of the American eagle, the ship of state, and other national symbols.*

into a secret society with the initials "K. F. R." The society began in a gardener's toolhouse on the grounds in 1871. It continued for more than half a century, though its name remained a secret. President Grant, observing some of its activities, once guessed that K. F. R. stood for "Kick, Fight, and Run."

Today, more than twenty sons and daughters of former Presidents—going back as far as Cleveland—live in various parts of the United States. Esther Cleveland, now Mrs. William S. B. Bosanquet, resides in Yorkshire, England.

In the summer of 1959, nine offspring of eight Chief Executives, plus nearly a score of descendants of Presidents beginning with John Adams, joined in a unique reunion at the Capital. The Women's National Press Club brought the group together for a nostalgic luncheon, followed by a tea and a tour of the White House with Mrs. Eisenhower.

Anecdotes exchanged that day ranged from comic to serious, as men and women recalled bygone incidents of "life with father." John Coolidge summoned up the dry humor of *his* father in a story of the time that the house barber knocked at the President's door and inquired if he needed anything before seeing the visiting Chief Justice, Charles Evans Hughes.

"No," said Mr. Coolidge, "but you might go down and ask the Chief Justice if he wants a shave."

ROBERT L. KNUDSEN

FRANK LESLIE'S ILLUSTRATED NEWSPAPER, APRIL 3, 1880, LIBRARY OF CONGRESS

"**HERE WE GATHER** *every evening," remarked President Hayes of the green-paneled library, today's Yellow Oval Room. Family and friends listen while Carl Schurz, Secretary of the Interior, coaxes "fantasias and caprices" from the keys. On Sunday nights, Cabinet officers and Senators joined in singing favorite hymns—"There is a land of pure delight," and "A few more years shall roll."*

PRESIDENTIAL ENCORE: *pianist Harry Truman begins one of his favorites, Paderewski's Minuet in G, for President and Mrs. Kennedy. As Chief Executive, he had played it for Prime Minister Churchill and Premier Stalin at a state dinner during the Potsdam Conference in 1945. Eugene List (right), then an Army sergeant, gave a Chopin program on that occasion and repeated it for Mr. Truman's White House evening in 1961.*

What the barber did is not recorded, but in view of Mr. Hughes's well-known pride in his luxuriant whiskers, the group got the point.

Grover Cleveland's son Richard and his daughter Marion Cleveland Amen represented the earliest President with surviving children. Mrs. Amen echoed the sentiments of the others when she said, "It's such fun to see . . . old friends." Her brother, born after their father left office, brought a laugh when he remarked that it was amazing how many people recalled seeing him play around the grounds.

Eleanor Wilson McAdoo wished to correct "the myth" that Woodrow Wilson had been "a very solemn man, an intellectual snob." On the contrary, she said, he was "our most amusing and gay companion."

Remembrance of past sorrow touched

the visitors when they came to the Lincoln Room, where, as John Coolidge pointed out, he and his younger brother Calvin had once slept.

In the summer of 1924, Calvin, just turned 16, had developed blood poisoning from a toe blister rubbed while playing tennis on a White House court. The best physicians of the day could not save him.

"He had a remarkable insight into things," Mr. Coolidge would write in his autobiography five years later.

"The day I became President he had just started to work in a tobacco field. When one of his fellow laborers said to him, 'If my father was President I would not work in a tobacco field,' Calvin replied, 'If my father were your father, you would.' . . .

"I do not know," Mr. Coolidge went on, "why such a price was exacted for occupying the White House."

Tragedy has indeed struck this bright home of success with appalling frequency. A nation and a family have grieved for eight Presidents who died in office—four of them, Lincoln, Garfield, McKinley, and Kennedy, at the hands of assassins.

The older Garfield boys, 17 and 15, would always remember with horror the morning of July 2, 1881. They and their father were expecting to join the rest of the family, vacationing at the seaside resort of Elberon at Long Branch, New Jersey.

They were in high spirits. Before leaving, the bookish President, who could turn handsprings as easily as he wrote Latin and Greek, engaged in a bit of competitive horseplay with his sons in their room.

PARTY GUESTS *masquerade as figures in American history at the first White House party given by Lynda Johnson, in August, 1964. In hoop skirt and bright silk ribbons, she appears as a Southern belle of the 1860's.*

GENTLEMEN *of the American Revolution, gamblers of the Mississippi riverboats, a gunman of the Old West—all join their hostess in the Entrance Foyer for a vivid tableau.*

A little later, as he was walking toward the main waiting room in the Washington depot of the Baltimore and Potomac Railway, an office-seeking fanatic fired two shots. One bullet grazed the President's arm and the other struck him in the back.

For 11 weeks, gravely wounded James Garfield – attended by helpless doctors under the anxious eyes of his wife and children – fought a brave, losing battle for life.

Frequent bulletins went out from the sickroom to the press and the public gathered at the mansion gates. The patient's condition had improved, worsened, then improved again. An effort was made to locate the bullet with a metal-detecting device offered by Alexander Graham Bell, inventor of the telephone. The attempt failed, probably because of the interference of the bed's steel springs.

Near the end, the President was moved, for a change of air, to the seaside resort where he had planned to vacation. He never returned to the White House. Instead his body was taken directly to the Capitol to lie in state. It was the only time in history that a Chief Executive who died in office did not lie first in the East Room.

Twenty years later, almost to the day, another psychotic killer shot President McKinley as he shook hands with a long line of people visiting the Pan American Exposition at Buffalo, New York.

In the special train rolling back to Washington, Ida McKinley, a small, bowed figure in black, sat beside her husband's body.

Of all the tributes paid him, perhaps the most unusual and poignant was one that accompanied a wreath presented in Buffalo by some seven hundred Indian braves and their chiefs who had taken part in the Exposition. President McKinley, they felt, had been a friend to the Indians. On a piece of pasteboard that served as their card, they had lettered this message: "The rainbow of Hope is out of the sky. . . . Tears wet the ground of the tepees. . . . The Great Chief of the Nation is dead. Farewell! Farewell! Farewell!"

Already a curious pattern, disturbing to the superstitious, could be noted in the passing of Chief Executives. From William

ROBERT L. KNUDSEN (BOTH)

◀ **PAGEANT OF PEACE:** *A brilliant star crowns a galaxy of lights on the National Christmas Tree.*

CHRISTMAS, 1939: *Four generations of the Roosevelt family gather by the tree in the East Room. The youngest, John Boettiger, Jr., examines the parquet floor. Great-grandmother Sara Delano Roosevelt sits beside the First Lady. Behind the President (from left) stand sons Franklin, Jr., John, and son-in-law John Boettiger. At F.D.R.'s right, Mrs. Franklin Roosevelt, Jr., holds Franklin III. To his left sit Mrs. Boettiger, Mrs. J. R. Roosevelt, and Mrs. John Roosevelt. Diana Hopkins, daughter of the Secretary of Commerce, shares the family's day, sitting on the floor between Presidential grandchildren Anna Eleanor and Curtis Dall.*

Henry Harrison (elected in 1840) to John Kennedy (1960), none of the seven men chosen at twenty-year intervals has lived to finish his Presidency.

Sorrow, personal and national, has been a too-frequent guest. Yet for every tear shed behind the great white columns there have been smiles of pride and joy.

"I have enjoyed myself . . . more than I have ever known any other President to enjoy himself," Theodore Roosevelt wrote to one of his sons near the end of seven ebullient years in the White House.

By all accounts, so had the rest of his family. After McKinley's somber administration, the eight members of the Roosevelt clan burst onto the scene in the fall of 1901 with the impact of a cyclone. The five younger children, aged three to fourteen, considered the house a playground. They slid down stairways on trays pilfered from the pantry, stalked halls on stilts, raced on skates across the East Room.

At various times, their pets included a badger, a bear, raccoons, rabbits, guinea pigs, cats, rats, dogs, snakes, and a calico pony named Algonquin. Algonquin gained the rare distinction of riding an elevator when the boys took him upstairs to comfort Archie, then in bed with measles.

After Quentin, the youngest, went to public school, he brought friends home to join in the fun. The hilarious adventures of this group fill a book called *The White House Gang*, written long after by one of its members, Earle Looker. It tells not only of the gang's irrepressible mischief, but also of the energy and humor of T.R., as the boys themselves called him, not in disrespect but with affection close to awe.

Whatever T.R. did—whether "dispensing justice" after the gang had spattered spitballs on Andrew Jackson's portrait, or taking on the boys himself for games in the attic—his understanding of small fry was phenomenal, and his word law to them.

During an attic chase, one boy suddenly turned off the lights, then heard a crash. The President's head had met a wooden post, frighteningly close to a nail about the height of his eyes. "I'm quite all right," he reassured the stricken gang. "But never, n-e-v-e-r, *never* again, turn off a light when anybody is near a post!"

OVERLEAF: N.G.S. PHOTOGRAPHER JOSEPH J. SCHERSCHEL; UNITED PRESS INTERNATIONAL (ABOVE)

T.R. had less success in disciplining his beautiful daughter Alice, who was 17 when he succeeded to office. Reporters called the high-strung, adventuresome girl "Princess Alice." She lived up to the title in a royal round of gaiety, and made it clear that her devotion to her father was equaled only by her desire to have her own way.

"I can do one of two things," the President said on learning of a new escapade. "I can be President of the United States, or I can control Alice."

Fortunately for all, the domestic head of this tumultuous menage, Edith Roosevelt, possessed the necessary calm, charm, and competence to keep both family and official life on an even keel. From one of her younger sons came a sincere, if confused, compliment to Mrs. Roosevelt's capacities. "When Mother was a little girl," he said, "she must have been a boy."

Such anecdotes tell us much of the activities and feelings of the changing families who have called the White House home.

One of the proudest of Presidents' wives was Mrs. William Howard Taft as she walked from the inaugural-day snow into the mansion's entrance hall on March 4,

1909. ". . . I could not help but feel," she wrote in *Recollections of Full Years*, "something as Cinderella must have felt when her mice footmen bowed her into her coach and four. . . . I stood for a moment over the great brass seal . . . which is sunk in the floor. . . . 'The Seal of the President of the United States,' I read around the border, and now—that meant my husband!"

The Tafts, however, were no strangers to the house. As old friends of the Roosevelts (the new President had been T.R.'s Secretary of War), they had often visited here. Their younger son Charles had been a member of Quentin's White House gang, and once when Quentin had been scolded for roughing up a room, he said, "It is all right, Mother. Charlie is with us, and it will soon be his house anyway."

In a sense, the Taft family belonged to two eras. It would be the last to keep a cow, called "Pauline Wayne," to give milk for the White House table, and the first to use a Presidential automobile.

Taft's successor, President Wilson, had often joked that no man made a great success "without having been constantly surrounded by admiring females." He, himself, proved the rule.

In the first year of his administration he spent happy, carefree hours as the center of a family circle made up of his fond, understanding wife and his three adoring daughters, Margaret, Jessie, and Eleanor.

A talented amateur artist, Ellen Wilson made their oval sitting room homelike with piano, books, and paintings brought from Princeton. Here, on many an evening before his wife's illness, the President would read to his womenfolk, or sing with them, while one of the daughters played the piano. Or he might recite a limerick, act the comedian, or dance a jig. If he hadn't gone in for politics, said Wilson, he could have had a vaudeville career.

Ellen's death, just as World War I began, threw Wilson into a deep depression. It lifted only after he met and fell in love with a vivacious Washington widow, Edith Galt.

Their meeting was a chance one. The President's cousin, Helen Bones, was entertaining Mrs. Galt at tea when the President returned unexpectedly from a golf game and joined them. In the months that followed Wilson courted the comely widow with flowers and poetry. He proposed to her on the South Portico, and announced their engagement from the White House in October, 1915. A quiet wedding took place at the bride's home shortly before Christmas.

From then on, devoted Edith Wilson stood at the President's side through America's participation in the war, his triumphant trip to Europe, and his devastating defeat in the League of Nations campaign.

Without her "love and care," Mrs. Wilson's social secretary, Edith Benham, wrote during the stressful period of early 1919, "I don't believe he could live."

From biographies, memoirs, and old news accounts come random, revealing sidelights on the families that followed the Wilsons at 1600 Pennsylvania Avenue.

In his easygoing, home-town way, President Harding called his strong-minded wife "the Duchess." Florence Harding told her friends, "I have only one real hobby—my husband."

Calvin Coolidge took great pleasure in

NATIONAL GEOGRAPHIC PHOTOGRAPHER JOSEPH J. SCHERSCHEL (BOTH)

SANTA CLAUS *presides over a party for 150 needy children in December, 1965. At right, his special assistant, Luci Johnson, plays hostess in the Red Room, carrying on a White House tradition that Andrew Jackson began with his Christmas gifts for Washington orphans.*

UNITED PRESS INTERNATIONAL

MOVIES AT HOME: *Mrs. Eisenhower watches a film with granddaughters (from left) Susan, Mary Jean, and Barbara Anne in the East Wing's ground-floor projection room.*

WHITE CHRISTMAS *at the White House arrived just two days late in 1939. Here, Roosevelt grandchildren "Sistie" and "Buzzie" Dall pelt one another with powdery snow. Earlier, they coasted on mounds built by Jefferson to screen part of the estate from public view.*

NATIONAL GEOGRAPHIC PHOTOGRAPHER JOSEPH J. SCHERSCHEL

ANOTHER SPACE WALK! *Col. Edward H. White II, first American to venture outside a capsule in orbit, tosses his daughter Bonnie into the White House pool. At his feet, Patrick McDivitt, son of his space partner Maj. James A. McDivitt, waits for the splashdown. President Kennedy's father commissioned the mural of St. Croix harbor in the American Virgin Islands.*

WIDE WORLD

ON HER FIRST DAY *at her new home, February 4, 1961, Caroline Kennedy finds a snowman waiting with Head Gardener Robert M. Redmond, who built him, Panama hat, coal buttons, and all.*

WORLD'S WORK, 1921

LADDIE BOY, *the Hardings' famous Airedale, shakes hands with the First Lady, offering her the wrong paw with irreproachable dignity.*

LIBRARY OF CONGRESS

PRUDENCE PRIM, *"the White House flapper," appears at a garden party in June, 1926. The white collie wears a bonnet trimmed with maidenhair fern and designed by Mrs. Coolidge.*

choosing hats and dresses for his amiable, gray-eyed wife. He favored bright colors and fancy trimming, and quite forgot his usual Vermont economy.

The scholarly, much-traveled Hoovers built bookcases along the wide family corridor, and filled them with works on the Orient, geology, and sociology, plus volumes presented to the White House by booksellers of America. At the west end of the hall, Mrs. Hoover created a pleasant, informal setting with wicker furniture, palms, and twittering caged birds.

But not since the boisterous tenure of Teddy Roosevelt had there been anything like the big and lively household set up in 1933 by another branch of this family, Franklin and Eleanor Roosevelt's. Their five children (three married and two in school) popped in and out, bringing offspring and friends to add to the commotion of F.D.R.'s eventful era.

In time, eleven more grandchildren joined famous "Sistie" and "Buzzie," as Anna Eleanor and Curtis Dall were known from coast to coast. And all thirteen of them saw Grandfather sworn in on the South Portico for his unprecedented fourth term in January, 1945—less than three months before he died of a cerebral hemorrhage in Warm Springs, Georgia.

The change of pace jolted the White House staff when the three Trumans quietly moved in after the great state funeral in the East Room. But it was not long before the new President, his wife Bess, and their 21-year-old daughter Margaret hit their own stride.

On the family floor stood three pianos—the President's, in the oval room used as his study, Margaret's, and a spinet in the hall outside her room. They made a fitting symbol for the trio from Independence, Missouri. Whatever the world might say, the team backed one another in everything from Margaret's singing career and Mrs. Truman's haircut to the President's whistle-stop campaign that rolled on to his re-election despite the pundits' predictions.

With President and Mrs. Eisenhower, the mood in the White House changed again. Now the pattern bore the imprint of popular General "Ike" and his wife Mamie, who played the role of First Lady with disarming naturalness.

After some 30 moves in 36 years of Army travels, the Eisenhowers lived longer in the Capital's big white house than they had in any other place. Whenever possible, they made the most of it in frequent visits by their grandchildren, watching TV programs, bridge games with friends, or a supper of steak or stew cooked by the President himself in the third-floor kitchen.

In the long family saga of the White House, there were never more appealing scenes in the private apartment than when John Kennedy and his glamorous Jacqueline spent happy times here with their children. Both parents believed in being with the youngsters as much as possible—playing with little John, Jr., perhaps, or making up imaginative stories for Caroline.

During the all-too-short time that her family was complete, Mrs. Kennedy once expressed this basic philosophy: "I feel that a woman should give half of her life to her husband, half to her children," she said, "and never let either one suffer."

FOLLOWING the Kennedy assassination, President Johnson, his wife, and their two daughters, Luci Baines and Lynda Bird, moved into the Executive Mansion on December 7, 1963. "We were all very gloomy," recalls Luci, who was 16 at the time. "It was only two weeks after the tragedy. It was the anniversary of Pearl Harbor . . . And on our first night I set fire to the place."

Actually it was not much of a fire. Luci and a young friend, in an effort to cheer things up, kindled a fire in Luci's bedroom. Smoke billowed out, and all the glasses of water the girls threw into the fireplace had no effect. Soon attendants came running and opened the damper that had caused the trouble.

The Johnson girls were the first teenage daughters (Lynda was 19) to come to the house since Helen Taft, more than half a century before. And like the other daughters, including Wilson's and Truman's, they soon found the public spotlight constantly focused on them.

Under a law passed in 1917, the Secret Service has kept a perpetual, protective eye on all members of the President's immediate family. An agent makes a threesome on Lynda's every date, and a special detail now guards Luci Nugent in her Austin home.

"With all this fuss made over us, we have to remind ourselves that we are really not very important," says Lynda. "I sometimes think of those Roman slaves I read about in my history lessons. They had to stand in

FRANCIS MILLER, LIFE © TIME INC.

HIM AND HER, *the Johnsons' beagles, warily inspect the second-floor hallway in 1964. Rarely permitted in the mansion, they usually romped near their own home on the south lawn.*

the chariot behind a general or emperor when he rode in triumph through the streets, and mutter, 'You are mortal, you are mortal.' "

The Johnsons, headed by their energetic six-foot-three husband and father, are an affectionate, demonstrative family. Like any other mother, Mrs. Johnson likes to share her daughters' successes, talk over their problems with them.

"My children," she has said, "are the pulse and heartbeat of the White House."

President and Mrs. Johnson have thrown open the family quarters to friends and visitors to an unparalleled degree. As host and hostess in their country's first residence, they take pride in giving their guests the grand tour of the historic rooms east of the oval chamber.

In the Rose Guest Room, with its canopied four-poster bed, have slept five queens: Wilhelmina and Juliana of the Netherlands, Elizabeth, the Queen Mother, and her daughter Elizabeth II of Great Britain, and Frederika of Greece.

On these occasions, except in the case of widowed Queen Wilhelmina, the husbands of the royal ladies stayed in the Lincoln Room across the hall. This room, now furnished with objects used in Lincoln's time, is to many the most interesting of all.

Lincoln, however, did not sleep here but at the other end of the same corridor. He met with his Cabinet members in this east

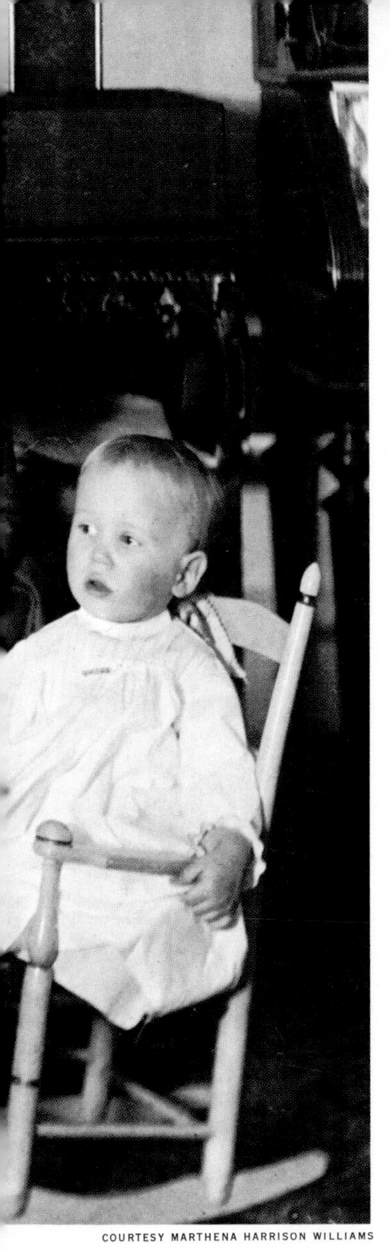

COURTESY MARTHENA HARRISON WILLIAMS

CLINEDINST PHOTOGRAPH, LIBRARY OF CONGRESS

MODELS OF DECORUM, *grandchildren of Benjamin Harrison enjoy a party in the second-floor nursery. Marthena Harrison reaches tentatively into a bowl, Mary McKee tastes a cookie, and Benjamin ("Baby") McKee watches from his rocker. Presiding: the President's daughter, Mrs. James Robert McKee (left), and his daughter-in-law, Mrs. Russell B. Harrison.*

WITH MAGIC WAND, *a fairy hostess accepts a bouquet. Mary Fairlie Tyler, the President's granddaughter, extends her thanks for a present on her third birthday. One of her guests, the inimitable Mrs. Madison, stands behind her.*

PRESIDENT WILSON *fondly cradles his first granddaughter, Ellen Wilson McAdoo, in 1915.*

PRESIDENT LINCOLN *turns the pages of a photograph album for his son Tad, February 9, 1864. At night, Tad would visit his father's office to report on his day's adventures, sometimes falling asleep beside the cluttered desk.*

room, and here he signed the Emancipation Proclamation.

The next-door Treaty Room, redone in heavy Victorian furniture and dark green walls, was once Lincoln's office. Andrew Johnson made it his Cabinet Room, a practice followed by other Presidents until the West Wing provided the needed space.

The present First Lady regards the Treaty Room as more of a museum than a family area. But she has known it to give practical service. When Lynda attended George Washington University, its massive table was often littered with chewed pencils and dog-eared books.

Living with history, the children of Presidents sometimes find, offers problems as well as incentives to learning.

Lynda and Warrie Lynn Smith, her visiting roommate from the University of Texas, once shared a room above the North Portico, below which early-morning visitors served as a built-in alarm clock. The chatter of tourists through the morning—"Now stand here, Johnnie, so I can take your picture; come here, Mary, don't fall in Mr. Truman's boxwoods"—forced the girls to decamp to the soundproof ground-floor theater to study.

ATTEN-SHUN! *The White House police line up for roll call; volunteer Archie Roosevelt gives the salute, volunteer Quentin stands at ease. From his office, T.R. could watch his youngest boys on duty—or hard at work in their sandbox.*

"**MY HOUSE,**" *John, Jr., called the President's massive desk. He liked to hide behind its secret door until someone knocked and asked, "Is the bunny rabbit there?"—and then, surprise! The best hour for this was shortly before his bedtime.*

LIBRARY OF CONGRESS

STANLEY TRETICK, LOOK MAGAZINE © COWLES COMMUNICATIONS, INC.

IV

The President at Work

THE PRESIDENT of the United States stands today at the control center of a vast, pulsing network of activities extending throughout the country and around the globe.

He heads a civil government of two-and-a-half million employees, and serves as Commander in Chief of U. S. military forces. From his administrative pinnacle, he oversees the spending of an annual national budget that has come to total well over one hundred billion dollars.

Whether he is traveling by plane, sitting in his office, or reading late reports in his bedroom, the President has only to press a button, pick up the phone, and be in instant touch with his Cabinet, legislators, ambassadors, or military leaders from Washington to Moscow to Southeast Asia.

His immediate staff at the White House averages about 250 men and women, most of whom are on duty in the West Wing. Among these are press and appointments secretaries, assistants, consultants, and aides—plus the essential office forces.

In addition, there are hundreds of other employees, stationed in the next-door Executive Office Building, who work for special staff agencies advising the President on traditional problems such as the budget, or on new ones such as space research.

And a modern Chief Executive needs all this assistance to provide the information and background he must have to reach decisions that only he can make.

It is hard to believe that less than 75 years ago, President Cleveland wrote much of his correspondence and many of his speeches in his own hand. Less than 50 years ago, President Wilson often picked up a letter from a secretary's desk and pounded out a reply on his own typewriter.

Such comparisons do not mean that the Chief Executive has ever had time on his hands. Even before the government moved to Washington, John Adams complained to his wife that a "peck of troubles in a large bundle of papers, often in a handwriting almost illegible, comes every day. . . . there is no pleasure."

Adams's son, John Quincy, used shorthand to cope with *his* paperwork a quarter-century later. But no copyist could read it, and the President wrote so many thousands of words in official and personal correspondence that both his eyes and his handwriting showed the strain.

By the time of James Polk, executive chores—multiplied by the Mexican War and later by the burning question of admitting new states as free soil or slave—laid a crushing burden on the President. The conscientious Polk wrote in his diary, "I prefer to supervise the whole operations of the government rather than entrust the public business to subordinates. . . ." And so he did in the period of America's greatest westward expansion, though it forced

CARES OF STATE *engross Mr. Johnson and Secretary of Defense Robert S. McNamara, pacing the mansion's West Wing colonnade. Herbert Hoover defined the scope of the Presidency: It "touches the happiness of every home. It deals with the peace of nations." John Adams wrote to George Washington in May, 1789: The Presidency "has no equal in the world."*

HARRIS & EWING (BELOW) AND NATIONAL GEOGRAPHIC PHOTOGRAPHER JOSEPH J. SCHERSCHEL

"**OUR BUNKER HILL** *of tomorrow may be several thousand miles from Boston," warns Franklin D. Roosevelt in May, 1941, as war in Europe threatens the U. S. He speaks in the East Room, scene of episodes as varied as Mrs. Adams's wash-days and F.D.R.'s fireside chats.*

"**THE AMERICAN DREAM** *for outer space is a dream of peace." President Johnson discloses plans for a manned orbiting space laboratory at his televised press conference of August 25, 1965. The aluminum framework above him added enough lights for motion pictures in color.*

him to labor day and night at his desk.

Once, after permitting a juggling act in the East Room to amuse Mrs. Polk's visiting nieces, he observed solemnly, "It was . . . innocent in itself, but I thought the time unprofitably spent."

Civil War emergencies brought more work and more help. Earlier Presidents had hired a private secretary, generally a family member who could be trusted with political and personal secrets.

President Lincoln had two secretaries, but was still "about the busiest person in Washington," as a reporter put it. He arrived at his east-corridor office before seven o'clock in the morning, ready to receive a parade of government officials, war contractors, Union generals, soldiers' wives and mothers pleading for justice or favors—and anyone else with a problem that "Father Abraham" might solve.

Not the least of the wartime President's troubles was the horde of office seekers who haunted his reception room, hoping for often nonexistent posts. Quipped Lincoln after contracting a mild case of smallpox, "Now I have something I can give everybody."

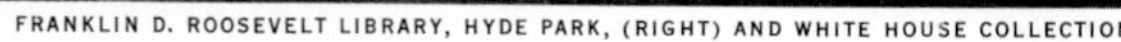

FRANKLIN D. ROOSEVELT LIBRARY, HYDE PARK, (RIGHT) AND WHITE HOUSE COLLECTION

Office seekers, however, had marked the American political scene since George Washington's day. Jefferson lamented that whenever he filled a post he gained "one ingrate and a hundred enemies."

Jackson frankly rewarded his supporters and announced a policy of dismissing avowed opponents. But he was not the spoilsman his detractors pictured. His replacements—sometimes for real cause—are now estimated at about one in ten.

Actually, the Presidents themselves suffered most from the system that long permitted office-hunters to harass the man in power. Applicants pursued William Henry Harrison during his short month of tenure. Surrounded by the pack on one occasion, he escaped only after stuffing his pockets and hat with their papers.

President Polk complained in his diary in 1847 that "neither ice nor fire" kept away the "herd of lazy, worthless people" who consumed his time. Moreover, he noted with dismay, they had grown so numerous they threatened to sway Presidential elections by holding "the balance of power between the two great parties."

Yet it was not until 1883 that Congress, aroused by Garfield's assassination, passed the first major Civil Service reform bill. This, the Pendleton Act, laid the foundation for making competitive examinations the basis for most Federal employment. In time, the Chief Executive would be able to bypass the ordeal of petty job appeals.

A BILL BECOMES A LAW: *In the Rose Garden by*

McKINLEY, *in his Cabinet Room, observes the signing of the Protocol ending fighting in the Spanish-American War. French Ambassador Jules Cambon (with pen) represents Spain; Secretary of State William R. Day, the U. S.*

DECEMBER 8, 1941: *F.D.R. signs the Declaration of War against Japan, the day after Pearl Harbor. He wears a mourning band for his mother, who had died that autumn.*

FIFTIETH STAR: *Eisenhower displays the nation's new flag after proclaiming the admission of Hawaii as a state on August 21, 1959.*

NATIONAL GEOGRAPHIC PHOTOGRAPHER JOSEPH J. SCHERSCHEL (BELOW) AND UNITED PRESS INTERNATIONAL

his office, on July 23, 1965, Mr. Johnson signs an Act of Congress changing the coinage of silver.

FOCUS ON VIET NAM: *Members of Congress hear Secretary of State Rusk at a White House briefing in March, 1965. The President, the Vice President, and the Secretary of Defense shared in the special report, using charts and a map to underscore key points. The Blue Room, normally a place for social gatherings, became a conference chamber for this and similar meetings.*

The President's House would remain the people's house, subject to their will, and open to their visits under varied conditions. But the nation was growing up. On its way to becoming the world's leading economic and military power, it could hardly expect its supreme chief to be accessible to anybody who chose to call.

In their West Wing offices—the nerve center of executive action since 1902—20th-century Presidents have carried on in a world of ever-accelerating pace.

Theodore Roosevelt, for all his restless energy, had only horseback and bicycle messengers to carry papers between the White House, Congress, and government offices. For himself, it was horse-and-carriage for local transport, and Pullman railway car for distance.

The White House stables—part of the establishment since Jefferson's day—gave way to an automobile garage in Taft's time. President Truman used the first official airplane, a four-engine C-54, later replaced by jets for Presidential flights.

President Eisenhower introduced helicopters for short trips. Until the lawn's landing area was moved farther from the South Portico, the whirlybirds blew off hats and tumbled the hair of those standing by.

In the last six decades, a growing executive staff has reflected each national and global challenge faced by the United States. "There were only a dozen of us on the White House staff at the turn of the century," recalled Chief Mail Clerk Ira Smith, looking back on 50 years of service.

By the time of the Hoover administration—when office personnel numbered perhaps 75—Mr. Smith wrote, "Big-business methods had finally taken over. . . ."

Franklin Roosevelt's New Deal innovations and World War II needs pushed the staff to about 225 members. Among these were the Presidential assistants whose qualifications, said F.D.R., were "high competence, great physical vigor, and a passion for anonymity."

Meantime, the daily work load steadily mounted. During President Taft's term, one person took care of all his telephone calls. When the operator went to lunch, young Charlie Taft thought it great fun to man the switchboard. By the Eisenhower period, 11 operators, in shifts around the clock, received an average of 7,000 calls a day. Now operators take some 10,000 daily; direct dialing brings countless others.

Nothing has been more spectacular than the rise of White House news coverage. T.R. provided the first official press room. According to an old story, he set it up in his new West Wing after seeing reporters shivering outside the gate one winter day.

By latest count, 25 representatives of

NATIONAL GEOGRAPHIC PHOTOGRAPHER JOSEPH J. SCHERSCHEL

newspapers, magazines, wire services, radio, and television are assigned, full time, to the newsroom off the West Lobby. From here they follow the President's every move, interview visitors, and respond to the summons for press conferences.

These question-and-answer conferences —initiated by Wilson—have taken many forms. They range today from scheduled televised meetings, attended by the entire Washington press corps, to impromptu walks around the grounds while President Johnson talks with the reporters on hand.

Many Chief Executives have expressed strong feelings concerning the office. Wilson said that the Presidency required "the constitution of an athlete, the patience of a mother, the endurance of an early Christian." "There will be no easy matters that will come to you," outgoing President Eisenhower warned John Kennedy. "If they are easy, they will be settled at a lower level." Coolidge once remarked that his job was like "the glory of a morning sunrise—it can only be experienced—it cannot be told."

Every President, however, meets his obligations by methods that stamp his personality forever on executive history. Mr. Johnson, for instance, has made unparalleled use of the residence as a symbolic stage and forum from which to launch and dramatize national programs and aims. Before TV cameras and distinguished

NATIONAL GEOGRAPHIC PHOTOGRAPHER JAMES P. BLAIR

guests he signs many Acts of Congress in the East Room and Rose Garden. In both, he installs officials and presents medals for major achievements.

Mrs. Johnson has added a woman's touch to "Great Society" projects. On one busy morning in 1965, she met with six social and welfare groups in five different White House rooms and one of its gardens.

Lady Bird (the unshakable nickname since childhood for Claudia) Johnson gives priority to two programs: beautification of America's cities and its countryside, and "Head Start," a nationwide effort to help preschool children of poorer families catch up with more fortunate youngsters.

Like Eleanor Roosevelt, Mrs. Johnson thinks nothing of flying across the country to further these and other goals, or taking off, say, to give a commencement address at a college in the Virgin Islands. Returning to the White House, she faces piles of mail arriving at the rate of a thousand letters a week. "Whenever I approach my desk," she says, "it erupts."

"IS THE PRESIDENT HERE TODAY?" *"Where does the family live in the house?" Historian Katherine E. Tippett (in Park Service uniform) answers these and many other questions for visitors at the mansion. The First Lady suggested this service in 1965. Now, from early May until Labor Day, two girls share duty at the North Portico (above) and the East Gate during tour hours, Tuesday through Saturday.*

SIGHTSEERS' LINE *at the White House fence becomes an impromptu receiving line as the President and the Vice President turn aside from a stroll in the grounds to shake hands.*

PERLEY'S REMINISCENCES

NEW YEAR'S DAY, 1866: *Paying their Chief Magistrate the compliments of the season, citizens stream into the Blue Room to shake the hand of President Andrew Johnson.*

LIBRARY OF CONGRESS, MAY 17, 1922

Circus giant George Augur with midgets Harry and Gracie Doll

LIBRARY OF CONGRESS, MARCH 10, 1925

Chiefs of the Sioux nation and President Calvin Coolidge

WIDE WORLD, MAY 20, 1921

Madame Curie with President Harding

Democracy's open house

CALLERS FROM MANY WORLDS have found hospitality at the White House. In 1874, King Kalakaua of the Sandwich Islands (now Hawaii) called on Ulysses S. Grant, first U.S. President to receive a reigning monarch. Madame Curie, co-discoverer of radium, visited Harding—who also greeted a circus giant and two small friends, movie stars Dorothy and Lillian Gish, and evangelist Billy Sunday. Coolidge's impassive face rivaled those of Sioux chiefs who came in 1925. In the next administration, Hoover presented the National Geographic Society's Gold Medal to pilot Amelia Earhart. The Franklin Roosevelts received the first British rulers to visit the former colonies, and, like Truman and Eisenhower, invited world leaders from Europe and Asia. The Kennedys' interest in the arts brought cellist Pablo Casals to the mansion for the first time since 1904, when he played for Theodore Roosevelt.

Mrs. Kennedy and Pablo Casals

© 1961, 1964 BY MARK SHAW, NOVEMBER 13, 1961

Britain's Queen Elizabeth, wife of George VI, and Mrs. Franklin D. Roosevelt

KEYSTONE PRESS AGENCY, JUNE 8, 1939

LIBRARY OF CONGRESS, DECEMBER, 1874

King David Kalakaua of the Sandwich Islands

HARRIS & EWING, MARCH 27, 1922

Dorothy Gish, David Wark Griffith, Lillian Gish

LIBRARY OF CONGRESS, FEBRUARY 20, 1922

Evangelist Billy Sunday

WIDE WORLD, DECEMBER 16, 1956

President Eisenhower greeting Jawaharlal Nehru, Prime Minister of India

ana Hopkins, Fala, Winston Churchill

HARRIS & EWING, JANUARY 3, 1942

Truman with General de Gaulle

HARRIS & EWING, AUGUST 22, 1945

Hoover and Amelia Earhart

ACME, JUNE 21, 1932

Few First Ladies have played so active a role as has Mrs. Johnson. Earlier wives have taken a keen interest in politics and judged political issues astutely—women like brilliant, ardent Abigail Adams, whose husband had wooed her as "Miss Adorable." But they discreetly kept their opinions within the family.

If they expressed thoughts on public issues, they confined themselves to mild support of such causes as temperance and humanitarian works. In 1815, Dolley Madison helped found an orphanage, and served as its "first directress" until her husband's term expired.

But Presidential wives have had their influence on the course of history. Sarah Polk's intelligence and education made her a priceless asset as private secretary to diligent James Polk. And President Hayes once remarked, "Mrs. Hayes may have no influence with Congress, but she has great influence with me."

When gentle Ellen Wilson came to the White House as the President's first wife, in 1913, she was so shocked by the squalor of Washington's back alleys that she urged her husband to propose a slum-clearance measure to Congress. She learned just before her death that the bill would pass.

But it was Eleanor Roosevelt, with her farflung public service, who made the President's wife a national force. She became the first First Lady to hold press conferences. Her regular meetings with Washington women reporters yielded prime news. Though she traveled as her crippled husband's "eyes and ears," her own lectures, writings, and welfare committees, her help to the unemployed, and her visits with overseas troops during the war, added up to a major career.

"For gosh sakes, it's Mrs. Roosevelt" was the caption on one timely magazine cartoon that pictured her surprising a group of coal-blackened miners on the job.

Every President's wife finds a ready-made career, however, when she steps behind the familiar white columns. And being mistress of the mansion, she soon learns, has problems and privileges that set this home apart from all others in the land.

ROBERT L. KNUDSEN (RIGHT)

IN THE NATIONAL INTEREST, *each Chief Executive consults spokesmen of both political parties. Above, President Johnson meets with former President Eisenhower and Republican Everett Dirksen, Senate Minority Leader.*

SECRET REPORTS *from key agencies and advisers often await Mr. Johnson's attention at night, along with other papers. "Of course," Mr. Eisenhower once observed, "the duties of the President are essentially endless."*

V

Behind the Scenes

FROM THE OUTSIDE, the President's House appears charmingly and deceptively modest. Except for unobtrusive office wings, it remains in structural outline just as it looked when it was basically completed in Jackson's day.

Inside, however, extraordinary changes have occurred. As a result of its 1948-52 reconstruction, the mansion contains 68 rooms by official count, with another 82 in the wings. Its facilities include a solarium, barbershop, movie theater, swimming pool, offices for a physician and a dentist, and a bomb shelter.

The kitchens, opening off the wide, arched corridor of the ground floor, display what one would expect of a chef's domain that produces four-course state dinners for as many as 200 at one time, and hors d'oeuvres for 5,000 reception guests. Within its gleaming white and stainless-steel rooms stand mixers, choppers, grinders, slicers, juicers, coffee roasters, electric ovens, and walk-in freezers.

In her wildest flights of fancy Abigail Adams could never have imagined such a transformation from her drafty, unfinished "castle," whose huge, empty rooms and halls lacked the basic household aids.

With enough candles "lighting the apartments, from the kitchen to parlors and chambers . . . [and] wood enough to keep fires," Mrs. Adams wrote her sister, "I design to be pleased."

President Jefferson, accustomed to the comforts of his Virginia home, Monticello, devised ingenious appliances for his official residence. One of these, a series of revolving trays built into the wall of his dining room (now the Green Room), brought in food and drink without the need of waiters.

"You need not speak so low," he once assured a guest made cautious by Europe's court spies. "Our walls have no ears."

Jefferson also added service wings on both sides of this building that a satirist of his time called "big enough for two emperors, one pope, and the grand lama." Their colonnaded fronts concealed workshops, a wine cellar, servants' quarters, ice- and meat-houses, even a lowly henhouse, in the areas used today for a swimming pool and TV and movie-projection room.

The greatest inconvenience in the earliest days must have been lack of running water. President Adams's servants had to haul water for cooking and bathing from springs nearly half a mile away, where Franklin Square is now. Jefferson installed a cistern in the attic, with a system of wooden pipes reaching through the floors.

In 1819 Congress appropriated money to pipe the spring water to the White House, but the project was not finished until 1833, in Jackson's second term.

Van Buren added a "reservoir" in the basement with a "double forcing pump" to supply the kitchen, pantry, and baths. His political enemy, Charles Ogle, made campaign capital by picturing the President's warm or tepid "Grecian Baths" as a luxury as decadent as the "palace's" gold spoons, derided in the same speech.

GLEAMING STEMWARE *passes a critical test—an inspection by food coordinator Mary Kaltman—as the hour approaches for a state dinner. These goblets, made in West Virginia, belong to a set chosen by Jacqueline Kennedy.*

NATIONAL GEOGRAPHIC PHOTOGRAPHER JAMES P. BLAIR

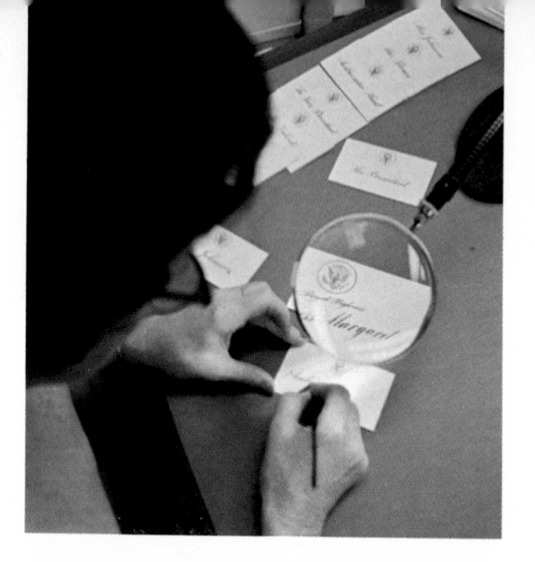

MARK KAUFFMAN, LIFE © TIME INC.

By 1855, the White House held a bathroom boasting a zinc-lined mahogany tub, and apparently no one objected. Theodore Roosevelt's renovation brought eight complete bathrooms. The present score for baths and washrooms adds up to 27 in the dwelling; 12 in the office wings.

With the advance of technology, other comforts of home followed one after another. Gas lighting was installed at the mansion in 1848, when only the Capitol and Pennsylvania Avenue were so illuminated. President and Mrs. Polk were the first to use the novel lights at a reception. That night the house was filled with guests when the "brilliant jets suddenly vanished." But darkness did not prevail everywhere. As Mrs. Polk liked to recall, she had kept the candles in the "elegant chandelier" of the East Room. There was "one room . . . still lustrous with many points of light . . . where the wax candles were shedding their soft radiance."

Until the Fillmores acquired the first kitchen stove, White House cooks had managed with a big open fireplace equipped with hooks, cranes, kettles, pots, and skillets. The new cast-iron contraption proved so confusing to the Fillmore cook that the President himself had to inspect the Patent Office model in order to give directions for operating its complex system of drafts.

Heating the mansion's open, high-ceilinged rooms has always presented prob-

WITH CLOSE ATTENTION *to the tiniest detail, the social staff prepares for a state dinner. The guest list compiled, Social Secretary Bess Abell (upper left in green dress) and an assistant arrange seating charts according to protocol. Then a White House calligrapher letters place cards for the President's tables.*

BEFORE DINNER *Mrs. Abell briefs White House social aides, young officers from each of the military services. After this meeting in the ground-floor library, they will greet guests at the south entrance and help them find their places in line for presentation to the President and First Lady in the East Room.*

IN THE STATE DINING ROOM, *Chief Usher J. B. West (left) confers with Head Butler John W. Ficklin long before guests arrive. Mr. West directs a staff of 72 domestic and maintenance employees at the White House. Here, he and the butler stand beside a table with settings of china used during the Lincoln administration and silver-gilt copied from Monroe's service.*

NATIONAL GEOGRAPHIC PHOTOGRAPHER JAMES P. BLAIR (ABOVE)

lems. As late as 1945, a news story told of the Trumans' having to call for portable electric heaters.

"Hell itself couldn't warm that corner," Jackson reportedly complained in the days of woodburning fireplaces, when residents burned on one side and froze on the other.

But nearly two more decades would pass before Franklin Pierce, in 1853, acquired the first central-heating plant, a coal-fueled hot-water and hot-air system that at last sent waves of warmth through the building.

It would have taken more than physical ease to dispel the gloom that enveloped Pierce's single term. "I have seen hundreds of log cabins that seemed to contain more happiness," a guest wrote in his diary.

The Pierce administration had begun under a cloud of personal grief that never lifted. Only two months before his inaugural, the President-elect and his frail, lovely wife Jane had seen their only remaining child, 11-year-old Benny, killed in a railway accident.

No inaugural ball was held. Mrs. Pierce was too shaken to come to Washington for several weeks. The President, after delivering his speech at the Capitol, and greeting long lines of handshakers at the White House, ended his first day in an incredibly forlorn setting.

The house grew dark; the servants had disappeared. Pierce and his private secretary, Sidney Webster, had to grope their way upstairs by candlelight and find rooms for themselves.

Throughout the Civil War and long after, the household conveniences at the White House lagged far behind those of fine private homes. Then, in 1877, President Hayes equipped the mansion with one of the first examples of an invention that would revolutionize American life—the "speaking telephone."

The President himself had taken part in a successful demonstration of the instrument arranged by its inventor, Alexander Graham Bell, between Providence and Rocky Point, Rhode Island. As Hayes, in Providence, listened to Bell's words coming from 13 miles away, a reporter noted that "a gradually increasing smile wreathed his lips and wonder shone in his eyes more and more. . . ."

It was President Arthur who put in the first elevator. Benjamin Harrison, with some misgivings, introduced electric lighting. "The Harrison family were afraid to turn the lights on and off for fear of getting a shock," wrote Ike Hoover, who came in 1889 to install the system, and who stayed for 42 years—most of them as Chief Usher.

With each added facility, more pipes, flues, and wires pierced the mansion walls. Successive structural changes weakened its basic supports. Ghost stories of knocks and footsteps heard in the night multiplied as floors sagged and ceilings cracked.

The unseen troubles of the house could no longer be ignored after President Truman noticed that the floor of his study shook at a single person's footsteps. In 1948, he and Mrs. Truman were greeting guests at a reception in the Blue Room when the heavy crystal chandelier above their heads shivered ominously.

An engineering survey made soon after revealed a shocking truth. The beloved home of American Presidents was about to tumble down. Backed by public clamor to preserve it, Congress authorized complete reconstruction within the original shell. Under the guidance of Maj. Gen. Glen E. Edgerton, executive director of the reconstruction commission, the building's interior was taken apart like a jigsaw puzzle, and put together again with the strongest supports available.

Below the restored ground-floor rooms workers built a basement and sub-basement equipped with a maze of technical devices to make the house that Fillmore described

PRESIDENTIAL BILL OF FARE *reflects the simple elegance of today's taste; in 1870 Ulysses Grant served 29 courses at a state dinner.*

MARK KAUFFMAN, LIFE © TIME INC.

as "a temple of inconveniences" into a comfortable, efficient place to live.

Above the family floor, the old attic where Teddy Roosevelt had romped with his children became a 14-bedroom annex for extra guests. The Coolidges' informal "Sky Parlor" returned as an air-conditioned solarium where Presidential families could continue to relax in privacy.

The new-old White House was completed in April, 1952, just in time for an overnight visit by Queen Juliana and Prince Bernhard of the Netherlands. But the kitchen was not yet ready to serve a full state dinner. So for this traditional entertaining, host Truman, like any other renovating householder, had to take his royal guests out to a hotel.

Each First Lady who crosses the threshold of the modern White House takes charge of an establishment that in many ways resembles a small well-run hotel.

She and her husband no longer hold the keys to their home. All their household needs in linens and tableware are supplied. The housekeeper does the family's personal marketing under the watchful eyes of a Secret Service man. Other food is bought in quantity and stored in freezers.

Nor does the President's wife, except in an over-all sense, need to worry about making her house presentable. For that she inherits a staff that now numbers 72 domestic and maintenance employees, such as butlers, waiters, cooks, maids, laundresses, carpenters, and plumbers. Atop the pyramid stands the Chief Usher, whose management duties include everything but ushering.

If such a staff seems large, consider a few of its tasks: 147 windows to wash; 600,000 square feet of wood floors to mop and shine; 15,000 square feet of carpet to vacuum, and some of the country's most valuable antiques to dust and polish daily.

Reflect, too, that the cleaning follows in the wake of some 40,000 visitors a week tramping through the rooms and halls, and that after each big dinner party comes the job of hand-washing perhaps a thousand pieces of crystal, two thousand pieces of fine china, and gold and silver flatware.

BUTLERS BRING SILVER TRAYS *and the chef ladles sauce over the roast squab for the dinner honoring Princess Margaret and Lord Snowdon.*

CHRISTMAS COOKIE FOREST *spreads before pastry chef Ferdinand Louvat. Mrs. Kaltman helps him create treats for a children's party.*

NATIONAL GEOGRAPHIC PHOTOGRAPHER JOSEPH J. SCHERSCHEL (BELOW)

Through the years, the President and the government have shared running expenses here in varying proportion. At first the Chief Executive paid all costs, except basic repairs and alterations, from his salary of $25,000 a year.

This sum seemed substantial then, but it was hardly adequate. Jefferson and Monroe had to sell land to meet the debts they incurred by entertaining in the style they felt essential to the new nation's dignity.

Jefferson's wine bill alone came to nearly $11,000 in his two terms. His grocery expenses in Georgetown often reached $50 a day. In Dolley Madison's Washington, prices were higher than elsewhere—75 cents for a turkey, $3 for a hog.

In Taft's time, Congress relieved Presidents of having to meet house-servant payrolls. Mr. Taft also was first to receive an annual salary of $75,000, an increase of $25,000 over that voted in 1873 and effective in Grant's second term. President Truman in 1949 was first to earn $100,000.

Recognizing the increasingly intolerable expense of official entertaining, the government has picked up the check for it since the Harding administration.

Presidents have continued, however, to pay family expenses—for personal maids and valets, family food and laundry, personal telephone calls, and private parties. The White House staff routinely separates these bills and those for such occasions as Luci Johnson's wedding so they cannot be confused with official costs.

With a century and a half of improvements rolled into one at the time of the 1952 reconstruction, it might have seemed then that the mansion was at last perfect. But there was still no dining room in the family's second-floor area. Meals had to be brought on trays, or the First Family had to go down to the private dining room on the semipublic floor. To meet the need, Mrs. Kennedy turned two second-floor rooms into a small kitchen and a charming dining room. The addition has proved so

useful that it is hard to see how earlier families did without it.

Certainly it was handy in June, 1965, when America's space heroes James McDivitt and Edward White came to Washington to be honored for their historic 62-orbit flight. Amid the proceedings, President Johnson unexpectedly announced that he was sending the astronauts on a goodwill mission to the Paris Air Show then in progress. Before leaving, the McDivitts and Whites were invited to spend the night in the White House.

"At two or three in the morning, we all pitched in to help them get off," recalls Mrs. Johnson. "Lynda was away. Luci ran the washing machine to freshen clothes for this surprise trip; she scrambled eggs, and made coffee. I brought out light coats and evening dresses from our closets to lend to the wives. It was quite a cooperative affair, and nobody gave a thought to lost sleep!"

FRANK LESLIE'S ILLUSTRATED WEEKLY (LEFT) AND NATIONAL GEOGRAPHIC PHOTOGRAPHER JAMES P. BLAIR

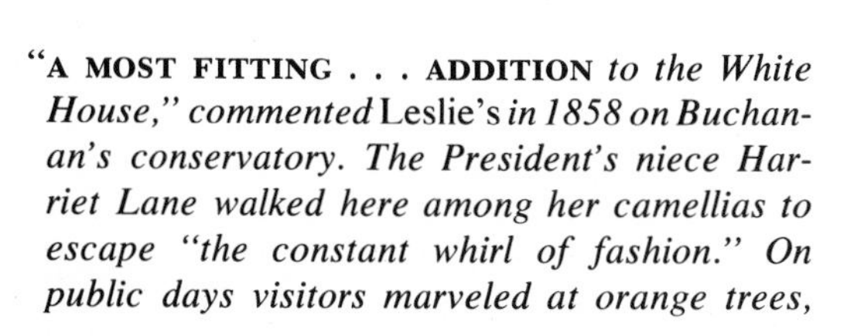

"**A MOST FITTING . . . ADDITION** *to the White House," commented* Leslie's *in 1858 on Buchanan's conservatory. The President's niece Harriet Lane walked here among her camellias to escape "the constant whirl of fashion." On public days visitors marveled at orange trees, aloes, and pitcher plants from South America. The old greenhouses west of the mansion came down in 1902, but the gardens still flourish. Above, Head Gardener Irvin Williams inspects a Chinese redbud tree, and Head Chef Henry Haller chooses a sprig of thyme from the herbary.*

IN SUMMER TWILIGHT, *guests at the 1965 White House Festival of the Arts dine on the south lawn*

VI Parade

NATIONAL GEOGRAPHIC PHOTOGRAPHER JOSEPH J. SCHERSCHEL

after a day of drama and exhibits. An outdoor program of ballet and music followed in the evening.

Ground and Playground

TO THE LITTLE BOY, flying was part of the fun of living in the big white house where something was always going on. Often the whirring helicopters would drop down into his own back yard, blowing up a stiff breeze. Sometimes they would take him to bigger craft that flew the family to other cities, other homes.

But the most exciting event for John Kennedy, Jr., and his sister Caroline came when the 'copters brought their father home. Sometimes the choppers introduced important strangers. Then round-eyed children could watch from a grandstand balcony as gun salutes boomed across the White House grounds, and troops in dress uniform paraded to martial tunes.

Though the youngsters could not have known it, the acts they saw were only the latest played on an outdoor stage that forever changes props and actors. Back in 1911, a pioneering pilot landed a Burgess-Wright biplane on the south lawn to receive a gold medal from President Taft for a record-making cross-country flight.

The whirlybird transport initiated by President Eisenhower became a regular feature of President Kennedy's welcome for visiting heads of state. And President Johnson has continued to use this modern, scenic approach to America's Executive Mansion in its handsome green setting.

Such a setting did not grow overnight. On a visit in 1841, British novelist Charles Dickens found the grounds laid out in garden walks that were "pretty and agreeable" enough, but had "that uncomfortable air of having been made yesterday."

Dickens's remark was a little unfair to the mansion's first nine masters, who had tried to cultivate and beautify their surroundings—often with an unsympathetic Congress holding on to the purse strings.

Even before John and Abigail Adams arrived, a member of the President's Cabinet wrote one of the District Commissioners requesting that the "large, naked, ugly looking building" be provided with a fence

ROBERT L. KNUDSEN (LEFT) AND NATIONAL GEOGRAPHIC PHOTOGRAPHER JAMES P. BLAIR

BRAIN TRUST OF TOMORROW: *Presidential Scholars from every state mingle on the south lawn during award ceremonies in 1964. Composer Leonard Bernstein, who served on the commission to select the outstanding high school graduates, talks with an informal group.*

"**MORE THAN A MEDALLION** . . . *I bring you the pride and hope of a nation," declared Mr. Johnson as he presented the 1966 awards. The Chief Executive established the program in 1964 to honor the "most precious resource of the United States—the brain power of its young people."*

GRANDCHILDREN *of Benjamin Harrison await a ride on the lawn. Baby McKee drives His Whiskers, Marthena Harrison hangs on, and Mary McKee holds Uncle Russell Harrison's hand.*

CAROLINE KENNEDY, *riding the first White House pony since T.R.'s time, canters briskly across the grass in June, 1962, not far from Macaroni's stable on the south grounds.*

UNITED PRESS INTERNATIONAL (BELOW) AND LIBRARY OF CONGRESS

HARPER'S WEEKLY (ABOVE) AND LIBRARY OF CONGRESS

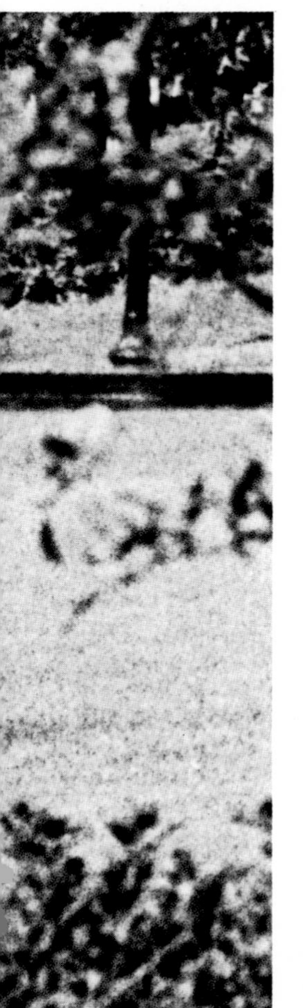

PRESIDENT GRANT'S SON *Jesse always remembered the "many contented hours" he spent at the brick stable. Begun in 1864, completed in 1867, it was demolished four years later when Congress designated the site for executive offices. At center, an orderly holds Grant's favorite Thoroughbreds, the matched bays Cincinnati and Egypt.*

SHEEP KEPT THE LAWNS *nibbled to neatness during World War I, while security measures closed the grounds to the public. "White House wool" from the flock, sold at public auctions, raised money for the Red Cross; its officials wrote to President Wilson in July, 1919, thanking him for "the very large contribution" of $49,333.57.*

FRANK LESLIE'S ILLUSTRATED WEEKLY, APRIL 23, 1887, COURTESY GRAY LINE INC.

TUMBLING AND RACING *down a hillock, children romp on the south lawn during the Easter Monday egg-roll in 1887. President Cleveland left his work to watch from his office window, noted a reporter, as boys and girls poured into the grounds, "armed with baskets of eggs dyed all the colors of the rainbow. . . . They rushed, scrambled and rolled for the oval prizes, which, when the shells broke under the rough usage, were eaten without more ado."*

and "something like a garden." "Would you not be ashamed," asked the letter writer indignantly, "to conduct the Pres^t to the House without there being an enclosure of any kind about it."

As we know, the request went unfulfilled. President Jefferson built the first fence, a straggling post-and-rail affair that blended well with the rustic look of a village where, as the secretary of the British Legation observed, "Excellent snipe shooting and even partridge shooting was to be had on either side of the main avenue. . . ."

Later, Jefferson replaced the wood fence with a fieldstone wall having an arched gate on the north. On the south, he earned the lasting gratitude of future families by grading the land and raising low mounds, thus leaving a view toward the Potomac, and at the same time giving the area some privacy.

More important at the time, Jefferson used his 18-acre estate as a holiday parade ground—especially on the Fourth of July. These gatherings, attended by throngs from neighboring "George Town" and Alexandria, were grand occasions in a community that still lacked the more sophisticated amusements of larger settlements.

It was not until some 20 years later, however, that the dour New Englander, John Quincy Adams, made the "President's Park" bloom with extensive flower and vegetable gardens. He also planted scores of fruit and nut trees.

Like all ardent gardeners, Adams collected seeds and seedlings wherever he went. Mingled with accounts of political successes and crises in his diary, we read that he plucked his pungent herbs as they came up—"balm and hyssop, marjoram,

NATIONAL GEOGRAPHIC PHOTOGRAPHER GEORGE F. MOBLEY (LEFT) AND UNITED PRESS INTERNATIONAL

COSTUMES CHANGE, *customs don't: squeals and a few small squabbles marked the celebration in 1963. When Congress banned egg-rolling on Capitol Hill, the Hayeses welcomed youngsters to the White House lawn.*

EASTER PARADE, 1953: *With baskets of eggs and clothes befitting the day, the Eisenhower grandchildren pause in the sun during a stroll with their mother, Mrs. John Eisenhower. From left: David, Susan, and Barbara Anne.*

mint, rue, sage, tansy, and tarragon." We learn of his delight that the "snowy medlar is showing a head of white blossoms," and the "roseate hue of the peach-blossom is just bursting out. . . ." And we share his distress that a hailstorm battered his nursery trees, and "lacerated piteously most of their tender leaves."

". . . the plants which I most cherish," he once said, "are the most apt to disappoint me and die." And, indeed, there remains only one of all Adams's trees—an American elm that spreads grandly above the lawn southeast of the mansion.

As the village Capital grew up, the President's Park acquired a more elegant air. From the 1830's on, professional landscape architects, including America's pioneering horticulturist Andrew Jackson Downing, laid out shrubbery, flower beds, and walks.

By the mid-19th century, the grounds, open weekdays to the public, had become a popular outing place. Every Saturday afternoon the Marine Band would present a concert—an already rooted tradition that would last until the turn of the century.

The *United States Magazine* for September, 1856, noted that "iron cottage seats scattered around, the view toward the stream and the breeze from the water makes this one of the most agreeable promenades in Washington. . . ."

A low ornamental iron fence, built near the mansion's north entrance in 1833, lent a fancy touch to the scene until it was torn down in the Roosevelt renovation of 1902.

At the same time, Grant's high gilt-tipped iron fence, built around the estate in 1870, gave way to a plainer one, in line with President Roosevelt's plan to

HURRAH, BOYS, HURRAH! *Abraham Lincoln, Commander in Chief, reviews a regiment of the three-year volunteers he called to service in 1861. Beside him, staunch in spirit but too feeble to stand, sits Lt. Gen. Winfield Scott. The President reviewed his men often that summer, at the White House or at forts nearby, and reporters noted their determination "to stand by the government and the old flag forever."*

TO THE TAP OF DRUMS *and the skirl of pipes, the famed Black Watch—the Royal Highland Regiment—drills for President and Mrs. Kennedy, and for 1,700 underprivileged children of the Washington area. Mr. Kennedy welcomed the unit that fought "against us . . . in the War for Independence" and "with us on many occasions" since.*

NATIONAL GEOGRAPHIC PHOTOGRAPHER GEORGE F. MOBLEY

SKETCH BY ALFRED R. WAUD, 1861, LIBRARY OF CONGRESS

restore the simplicity of the Federal period.

Also swept away then—to make way for the new executive wing—were the old White House conservatories. Long a Capital showplace on public visiting days, these rambling, glassed-in buildings, with their labyrinthine aisles and warm, scented air, had dated from the pre-Civil War era.

At the suggestion of his niece and hostess, Harriet Lane, Buchanan built the first formal, elaborate greenhouse in 1857. From then on, no First Lady lacked fresh flowers or growing plants to deck her home and table.

Beginning with Miss Lane, many a mistress of the White House found the conservatories a quiet, fragrant retreat from social pressures. Working with garden trowel and pruning knife, Mrs. Hayes spent long, pleasant hours among her lilies and roses.

Caroline Harrison took time to cultivate several rare varieties of orchids, despite her other interests and the duties of a four-generation household. An accomplished watercolorist, she enjoyed decorating china with paintings of her favorite orchids. Out of her interest in the pieces used by earlier First Ladies grew the White House China Collection that has come to represent every Presidential family.

Most of the flowers for the house are now obtained from wholesale distributors and Park Service greenhouses. Two staff members prepare the arrangements in a small ground-floor room redolent of many blossoms. White House gardeners tend the flowers still grown on the place.

They also raise kitchen herbs in the Jacqueline Kennedy Garden, dedicated by Mrs. Johnson in the spring of 1965.

"The 35th American President and his First Lady . . . loved beauty," said Mrs. Johnson, "and they loved it in the sturdy American tradition of seeking the beautiful that is also useful. . . . The garden includes flowers not only to be admired but to be cut; herbs for the kitchen and a center lawn for croquet and children's games."

Within their sheltered acres, generations of White House youngsters have discovered a world of outdoor adventure.

On Easter Monday in most years since the Lincoln administration, and perhaps earlier, they have shared their playground with Washington's children for the traditional White House egg-rolling. So many boys and girls now take part there is hardly room to roll their bright-colored eggs.

President Hayes laid out a croquet ground near the mansion's South Portico. There, wrote a staff member, clerks as well as the family "used to spend an hour now and then in the cool fresh air over hard-fought games with mallet and ball."

Teddy Roosevelt had his tennis court, on which he waged vigorous contests with associates who were called his "tennis Cabinet." Across these broad lawns raced Harding's pet Airedale, Laddie Boy, retrieving golf balls for his master. Hoover's "medicine-ball Cabinet" tossed eight-pound balls before breakfasting under a spreading tree. Truman set up the first and only

horseshoe court. Eisenhower's putting green still reminds visitors that he once practiced here.

An ideal place to keep pets, the executive grounds have seen a parade of animals that would fill a Noah's Ark with ponies, rabbits, goats, ducks, pigs, raccoons, and other garden varieties of creatures that a warm-hearted family might collect.

Tad Lincoln made a pet of a turkey that relatives sent for the Christmas dinner in 1863. He named it Jack. When the cook prepared to kill it, the boy rushed in tears to his father. The President broke off a conference with a member of his Cabinet, listened to his son's plea, and wrote a formal reprieve for the turkey.

Both wild and domestic creatures lived temporarily in the President's Park. The public gazed in amazement at Jefferson's exhibit of grizzly bears brought back by the Lewis and Clark Expedition as examples of strange fauna in the west.

To the delight of passing citizens, President Taylor rewarded his famous warhorse Old Whitey by putting him out to graze on the White House grounds.

Wilson purchased a flock of sheep to crop the lawn during the manpower shortage of World War I. From the wool regularly sheared and auctioned off, he obtained $49,333.57 for the Red Cross.

Looking south from the mansion today, toward a crystal pool set amid well-kept green expanses, no one would ever suspect that this vista once caused fear.

GRAPE ARBOR PROVIDES A STAGE *for Mrs. Johnson and Mrs. Hugh D. Auchincloss, who share in dedicating the Jacqueline Kennedy Garden on April 22, 1965. The Kennedys planned the hedge-bordered retreat in the 18th-century style as a counterpart to the President's Rose Garden; Mrs. Johnson guided its completion. In Mrs. Kennedy's absence, Mrs. Auchincloss (at lectern) represents her daughter. After the ceremonies, Mrs. Johnson takes a glass of iced tea at a reception for members of the First Lady's Committee for the Preservation of the White House—and for the White House Historical Association, whose $10,000 gift financed the project.*

NATIONAL GEOGRAPHIC PHOTOGRAPHER JOSEPH J. SCHERSCHEL

SMOKING CANNON *thunder a 21-gun salute to King Faisal of Saudi Arabia, arriving in the Capital on June 21, 1966, for a three-day state visit. Standing on a raised platform beside President Johnson, the desert monarch wears the wide royal headband that distinguishes him*

NATIONAL GEOGRAPHIC PHOTOGRAPHER JAMES P. BLAIR

from his black-robed retinue. Facing the two heads of state, an honor guard on the south lawn presents arms. Chosen from all the military services, the men carry flags of the fifty states of the Union. Behind the King, a red carpet of welcome leads toward the White House.

When the President's House was new, the river flowed much closer to the south grounds. With the felling of trees upstream, the Potomac began to silt up. By the 1840's, reeking mud flats had formed, giving rise to gossip, after President Taylor's death in 1850, that their fumes were responsible.

The constant dampness from the stream, and the chills and fevers suffered by White House residents, forced various Presidents to flee to rented houses in hot weather. Van Buren leased a summer home in nearby Georgetown. Buchanan accepted the loan of a cottage at the Soldiers' Home, as did Lincoln when war crises permitted.

One of Lincoln's secretaries, left behind in the exodus, wrote a friend, "I am alone in the White pest-house. The ghosts of twenty thousand drowned cats come in at night through the south windows."

The unwholesome swamps were finally drained and filled in the 1890's. The Capital was beginning to behave like a metropolis, though a young reporter named Frank Carpenter noted that workers on the flats were in danger of being shot by hunters, who could still bag reed birds there.

The swamp reclamation may have promoted the popularity of White House lawn entertaining after the turn of the century. Early in their first term, the Theodore Roosevelts held a series of such festivals, inviting Cabinet families and other friends.

Some four thousand guests came to the Tafts' night garden party celebrating their silver wedding anniversary in June, 1911. The grounds blazed with lanterns and strings of lights, and Mrs. Taft later wrote happily that "a more brilliant throng was never gathered in this country."

In the summer of 1918, President Wilson put on the first of the veterans' lawn fêtes that have since been repeated nearly every year. The dainty tidbits usually served at teas were replaced by man-size sandwiches —another continuing practice.

But it was not until comparatively lately that the grounds came into wide use for executive as well as social functions. To an ever-increasing degree, Presidents Truman, Eisenhower, Kennedy, and Johnson have met with special groups in the Rose Garden, outside the Executive Office.

Indeed, Mr. Johnson has arranged so many summer ceremonies and conferences here that reporters commented on his sunburn. Attendants have set up 500 folding chairs in the garden, or—on rare occasions—several thousand on the south lawn for large-scale events, such as the President's party for the press.

Greater use of the grounds does not mean, of course, any slackening of precaution by the Secret Service, the arm of the Treasury Department that has been responsible for the safety of the President and his family since 1901.

To get past the 13 gatehouses set at the various entrances, visitors must have a pass or official clearance. Secret Service men guard these posts day and night, and special agents remain close to the President and his family at all times.

BACK in the days when the public could wander at will, these grounds saw some motley groups. They also witnessed some of the most dramatic moments in American history. For two days, April 10 and 11, 1865, jubilant crowds, singing and cheering over the fast-approaching end of the Civil War, surged across the lawns before the South Portico.

On the night of the 11th, Lincoln appeared at a window, outlined against candlelight, to give his promised address. It was a speech warm with compassion for the defeated foe, and strong with the promise of rebuilding a cruelly torn land.

As the President read his carefully prepared lines—shifting from a joyous introduction to the serious weighing of reconstruction problems ahead, his young son Tad scrambled at his feet to catch the used sheets falling from his father's hands.

"Another . . . another!" the boy said, delighting in his new game, while the crowd listened, "silent, intent, and perhaps surprised," an observer noted, at so generous a policy toward the South.

It is at such times that the White House seems most in character—at once nationally exalted and humanly familiar.

Perhaps this is why most Americans feel that, although the President may travel far, there is only one house in which he and his family can ever live—the symbolic home of the nation itself.

STREAMERS OF FIRE *etch the sky above the President's home following a dinner for King Faisal. On the north grounds, a lighted fountain raises a bright beacon against the soft glow of the North Portico as the living White House shares a historic night with the people.*

JAMES R. HOLLAND

Index

Illustrations references appear in *italics.*

PRINTED AND BOUND BY FAWCETT-HAYNES PRINTING CORPORATION, ROCKVILLE, MARYLAND

COLOR SEPARATIONS BY LANMAN ENGRAVING COMPANY, ALEXANDRIA, VIRGINIA

END PAPER: *In the East Room, the Prince of Wales bows at President Buchanan's public reception in 1860.*
LIBRARY OF CONGRESS